Maine Woods Woolies

30 Quick-to-Knit Sweaters for Children

Maine Woods WOOLIES

by
Helene Rush

DOWN EAST BOOKS/CAMDEN, MAINE

ISBN 0-89272-222-3
Library of Congress Catalog Card Number 85-52441

Design by Janet Patterson
Composition by Crane Typesetting Service, Inc.
Printed at Capital City Press, Inc.

5   4

Down East Books, Camden, Maine

Contents

To my parents, Denise and Emilien Marchand

Preface

Our homes aren't as warm as they used to be, in this time of energy consciousness. Even with the thermostats turned down little ones can be made cosy in easy-to-make knitwear. Being a mother of three, I know how nice it is to have a selection of knits on hand for my kids to wear on these cold mornings when the woodstove went out during the night. Unfortunately, it's usually hard to find child-size sweater patterns that can be worked up quickly—until now!

In the pages to follow you will find thirty quick-to-knit sweaters in sizes ranging from six months to twelve years. I have designed these patterns to use worsted and bulky weight wools only to speed up the knitting process. No longer will baby's sweater take as long as daddy's.

I give you patterns for sweaters your children won't outgrow before you get a chance to finish your project!

Acknowledgments

When I decided to write this book, I thought I was going to do it all myself. If I had, you probably would not be reading this now for I would still be buried in wool and patterns, trying to finish sometime in this decade. But because of all the people who literally lent me their hands, I can now put my needles to rest (well, maybe for a day or so!) and compose a proper thank-you for them.

My first thank-you must go to my good friend Susan Michaud, who so graciously volunteered her time and talent to take all the pictures in this book. It's no easy feat to manage and pose nine children, five of them under the age of four.

Next, thanks to all those little "models," who were so patient with us in putting up with so many clothes and location changes on a hot day. Thanks to Kelly Anne, Jonathan, and Benjamin Rush, Holly and Christopher Michaud, Dale Bendixen, Erica Rush, Meghan Davis, and Sarah Pierce—and to their parents, who so readily volunteered them.

Then, there are the knitters who were such great help in putting this book together on time. Their names appear next to the individual patterns and are listed here again: Theo Heald, Kathy Baker, Lana Bradbury, Susan Darneille, Joanne Hutchinson, Theresa Timmons, Suzanne Desrochers, and Rhoda Libby.

I'm also grateful to Martha Hall, of Yarmouth, Maine, for providing me with materials and for the moral support she gave me in voicing her eagerness to see this book finished. And to Juli Weeks, of the Yarn Barrel in Scarborough, Maine, for finding me some good knitters in a hurry.

And finally, thanks to Aimee Sandberg for spending part of her summer keeping her eye on my three children so I could work those precious few hours a day undisturbed.

Putting a book together is really a team effort. A little help goes a long way!

Getting Started

What Materials to Use

I am concerned about the misconception so many people have when it comes to buying yarn for children's clothing: that synthetic fibers are the only kind to use. I would like to convince you otherwise.

Several brands of machine-washable wool are on the market today that are soft to the touch (no complaints about itching) and come in a wide range of weights and colors. Several of the sweaters pictured in this book have been knit in such washable wool and some have already been washed several times. One in particular, which I knitted for my older son, now being worn by my youngest, has been tossed in the machine often, as you can imagine. I challenge you to find which one it is!

The other type of yarn I chose for this collection is the so-called Maine wool, such as the Bartlettyarns and Christopher Sheep Farm yarns. It is locally spun of 100 percent wool with some of the natural lanolin left in it. Not only is it water repellent, but I have found it to be very stain-resistant. It also is less likely to pick up odors. This Maine wool is especially suitable for outdoor garments and is sure to keep your children warm. It is very rugged and washes well. Again, I have washed some of the sweaters several times and they have retained their shapes and good looks. They also become especially fluffy once washed, as the fibers from the wool spring to life and fill in all the gaps between the stitches. The only thing you cannot do with 100 percent wool sweaters is machine-dry them. Just lay them flat and they should dry in a day or so.

Wool *does* cost more than synthetics, but what's "expensive" is only a matter of opinion. Using the Maine wool, a size 8 can be knit for under twenty dollars. My kids use their sweaters as spring and fall coats, and where can you buy a pure-wool coat for that little?

Then, there are also several types of wool-blend yarns on the market. They offer the added warmth of wool and the easy care of the synthetic fiber. These really are preferable to any 100 percent manmade yarn. Considering the hours you will spend on this project, don't you think you deserve to work with the best?

Here is a list of the materials I used for the sweaters in this book:

Bartlettyarns 2-ply and 3-ply Fisherman wool
Bartlettyarns 2-ply and 3-ply Homespun wool
Christopher Sheep Farm wool
Scheepjeswol Superwash Zermatt wool
Phildar Pegase wool blend
E'Lite Manhattan mohair
Textile Studios at Hoosuck 88Line/Trilla wool

All the materials and buttons I used may be obtained at:

> Martha Hall
> 46 Main Street
> Yarmouth, Maine 04096

Substitutions may be made by using the specific ounce quantities and yardage indicated on each pattern. I have tried to be generous in listing quantities to keep you from running out of wool before the project is completed. As with any knitting project, be sure to buy all your yarn from the same dye lot. Don't be afraid to buy one extra skein, especially if you intend to change the sweater dimension (longer than on the pattern, for example). Find out the return policy of the store where you are purchasing the materials. Most shop owners will let you return unused skeins if you kept your receipt and if it has not been too long since you made the initial purchase. Better to be safe than sorry!

Which Size to Make

Anyone who makes or buys clothes for children knows how hard it is to find the right fit. Unfortunately this has a lot to do with the infinite range of sizes children come in and the varying rates at which they grow. I have indicated the finished chest measurements for each size, and I'd advise you to select the size that will be at least two to three inches more than the child's actual chest size, more if you are making a garment that will be worn over something else.

The length can be easily altered if needed (check against another, well-fitting pullover for accuracy), but bear in mind, of course, that any changes will affect the yarn quantities for the project. It's better to make the sleeves on the long side, since children seem to have a habit of growing too fast. You can always turn up the cuff until the child grows into it.

The numbers used for identifying sizes do not necessarily indicate ages. For example, my daughter at age four is wearing a size 4 fitted pullover and a size 6 outdoor-type pullover.

I hope this will help you decide which size to make, but if, like me, you knit for your nieces who live in Canada and whom you haven't seen in two years, all the experience in the world won't help. What I send is always the wrong size!

What About Gauge?

Gauge, gauge, gauge! For those of you who have finally understood the importance of this five-letter word, you are allowed to skip this section! But to all others who are still wondering how come what they knit never ends up being the size it is supposed to be—read on.

Obtaining the correct gauge is a must. The patterns in this book were designed to be worked fast, but there is no worse way to waste your time and materials than to not take a little extra time to knit a test swatch. This swatch should be at least four inches square. Use the recommended needle size and multiply by four the gauge given for one inch to determine the number of stitches to cast on. Work back and forth in stockinette stitch (unless otherwise indicated). If two or more colors are used for the main part of the sweater, work your swatch following the color chart, as the gauge may change in these cases. Remove the stitches from the needle.

Lay the swatch flat on a hard surface and measure across. It should be four inches wide. If the swatch is too narrow, try the next larger size needles; if it is too wide, try the next smaller size needles. In general, the size of the four-inch swatch will change by $\frac{1}{4}$ inch with each increment in needle size.

The row gauge is also important in patterns with a raglan sleeve, where it will determine the depth of the armhole.

For an example of the importance of the gauge, take time to look at the Cabled Turtleneck and the Fair Isle Pullover patterns. Both these patterns have the same gauge of 4.5 stitches per inch, but one requires size 7 needles to obtain gauge, while the other one requires size 5 needles. The reason is that the yarn used in the turtleneck is a lighter-weight knitting worsted, while the pullover is made from Maine wool, a heavier type that still falls in the worsted weight category. The reverse is true in the case of the Penguin Pullover and the Rabbit Pullover. In both cases, size 5 needles are used but the gauges are different.

Since you may not knit with the same tension as the person who wrote the patterns, and since you may also be substituting yarns, the importance of obtaining the correct gauge in all knitting projects must be evident to you. So to *save time, take time* to always check gauge, gauge, gauge!

Special Techniques

A number of the patterns require you to use embroidery stitches, crochet stitches and special knitting techniques. Some of these may be new to you, so they are explained below.

French Knots

Using a yarn needle, draw yarn through where you want the knot to be, then wrap the yarn around the needle twice.

Insert the needle back into the fabric exactly where it just came out. Pull yarn through. There is your French Knot!

Duplicate Stitch

Draw yarn through fabric, from back to front, at the base of the stitch you want to cover. Pass needle behind the two strands that form the base of the next stitch above.

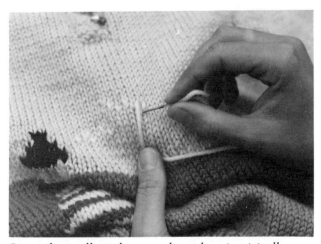

Insert the needle at the same place where it originally came out and pull yarn through to back. Repeat as needed.

One-stitch Buttonhole

Work to where you want the buttonhole to be, bring yarn to front of work, knit the next 2 stitches together, passing the yarn over the needle to accomplish this. Repeat as needed.

Single Crochet

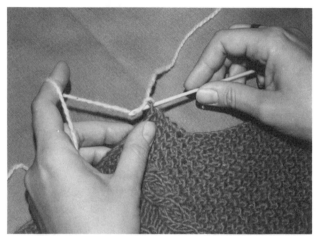

Step 1: Attach yarn where you want to begin crochet edge. Insert crochet hook through stitch on fabric edge and put yarn over hook.

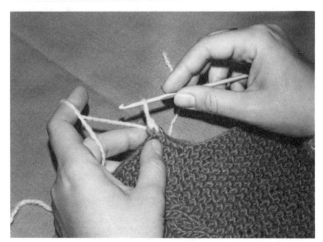

Step 2: Pull through to make a loop. Put yarn over crochet hook again and pull a second loop through the first.

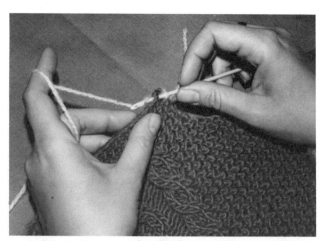

Step 3: Insert crochet hook in stitch next to first insertion. Put yarn over crochet hook.

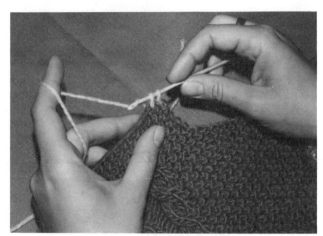

Step 4: Pull through to make another loop. Put yarn over crochet hook.

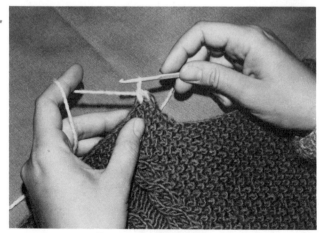

Step 5: Pull yarn through both loops. Repeat steps 3, 4, and 5 for single crochet.

Chain-2 Buttonloop

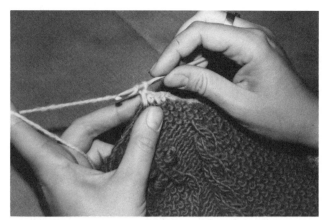

Step 1: Work in single crochet to the place where you want to make the buttonloop.

Step 2: Put yarn over crochet hook. Pull through a loop for chain 1. Draw through as many loops as required (i.e., chain-1, chain-2) to complete buttonloop.

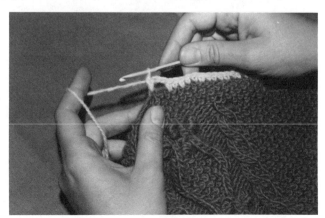

Step 3: Work in single crochet to complete the buttonloop, leaving a space between this and the preceding single crochet, as shown.

Knitting with Several Colors

Color knitting is not the easiest thing to do, but only practice will make you proficient in it. Following these tips will help you obtain satisfactory results.

When knitting with two or more colors, take care to not carry the strands of colors not in use too tightly across the wrong side of the work. Strands should be crossed every half inch to eliminate the possibility of small fingers getting caught in long loops (this really should be done in adult garments too). And you should always twist the two strands together once when dropping one color and beginning a new color to prevent making holes in the fabric.

In working snowflakes (also called chevrons) in which a contrasting stitch is knit in at regular intervals, across fabric every two or four rows, the following method may save you time in eliminating the sometimes tedious task of crossing strands every two or three stitches. Be careful to leave the tension fairly loose in the strands carried behind the work so that they will not pull when picked up on the next row.

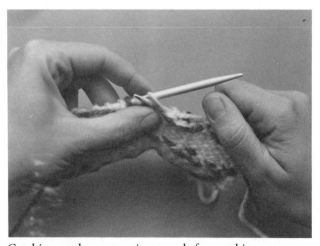

Catching up the contrasting strand after working pattern on a right-side row. *With wrong side facing you, work to the place where you want to catch up the strand. Insert the right needle in the next stitch purlwise, catching the contrasting strand from the row below at the same time.*

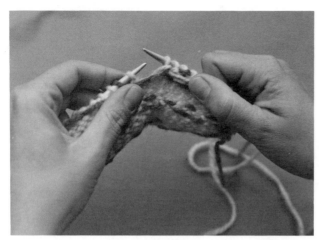

Purl the stitch as usual. The strand is now caught firmly in place. In the snowflakes pattern, the strand will be caught up once between each pair of snowflakes.

After working pattern on a wrong-side row: *With right side facing you, work to the place where you want to catch up the strand. Insert the right needle in the next stitch knitwise, catching up the contrasting strand from the row below at the same time.*

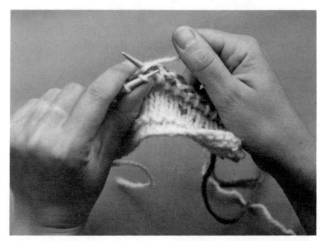

Knit the next stitch as usual. The strand is now caught firmly in place.

The Patterns

If you are like me, you skipped all the pages before this to get directly to the patterns! Of course I am happy to think that you are anxious to start working on your project, but please take the time to scan through the previous pages, which include tips you may find interesting or even indispensable.

I have provided sketches for all the sweaters to help you get a better look at the styles and stitches, and I have been careful in working easy-to-read full-width color charts of the design motifs. In these patterns I have used a lot of button closures at the shoulder and neck so you won't have to wrestle your kids into their sweaters!

Knitters who may be a little shy about using the multicolor charted designs can instead knit the garments in one solid color. I've provided several different styles for that purpose.

Throughout all the patterns, several common abbreviations have been used. Here are their meanings for those of you who may not be familiar with them:

st, sts = stitch, stitches
k = knit
p = purl
inc = increase, increasing
dec = decrease, decreasing
beg = begin, beginning
yo = yarn over the needle
k 2 tog = knit 2 stitches together
sl 1 = slip 1 stitch
psso = pass slipped stitch over the stitch just knitted
MC = main color
CC = contrast color

A Touch
of
Maine

Moose Pullover

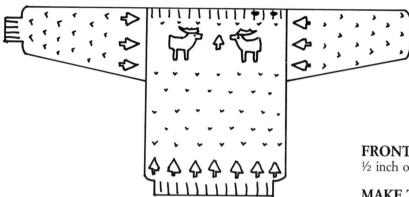

SIZES: Instructions are for size 12 months. Changes for sizes 2, 4, 6, 8, 10, and 12 are in parentheses. Finished chest measurements are 20 (22½–24½–25¼–26¼–28–30½) inches.

MATERIALS: 5 (6–7–8–9–10–12) oz or 265 (315–370–420–475–525–630) yds worsted weight Maine wool for color A; 2 oz or 100 yds (all sizes) for colors B and C. 1 pair each size 3 and size 5 needles, or size needed to obtain gauge. 2 ½-inch buttons.

GAUGE: 4.5 sts = 1 inch.

BACK: With size 3 needles cast on 44 (50–54–56–58–62–68) sts in color A. Work in k 1, p 1 rib for 1 (1½–1½–1¾–1¾–2–2) inches, inc 1 st in last row to make 45 (51–55–57–59–63–69) sts. Then, with size 5 needles, work in stockinette stitch (k 1 row, p 1 row) for 2 rows. Begin Chart 1, pine trees and snowflakes, continuing snowflakes as established until 7½ (8–9½–10–10½–11–11½) inches from beg. Place markers at both ends of needle for armhole. Work Chart 2, continuing snowflakes as established when chart is complete, until 3¼ (3¾–4–4½–4¾–5–5½) inches above armhole markers. Work in k 1, p 1 rib for 1 inch.

SHAPE SHOULDER: Bind off 9 (12–13–14–15–16–19) sts at beg of next row, place marker, bind off next 27 (27–29–29–29–31–31) sts. Continue on next 9 (12–13–14–15–16–19) sts in k 1, p 1 rib for 1 inch more for left shoulder extension. Bind off all sts.

FRONT: Work as for back until you have worked ½ inch of ribbing at shoulder.

MAKE TWO BUTTONHOLES: With right side facing, in established ribbing, work 1 (2–3–4–4–4–6) sts, k 2 tog, yo, work 1 (3–2–3–4–4–6) sts, k 2 tog, yo. Work on to end of row in ribbing as established. Work on all sts in ribbing for ½ inch more. Bind off all sts.

SLEEVES: Sew right shoulder seam to neck opening marker. Overlap left front over left back at shoulder and slip-stitch 1-inch overlap at armhole edge. With right side facing, using size 5 needles and color A, pick up and k 39 (43–45–51–53–55–59) sts on armhole edge between markers. Purl back. Work Chart 3, continuing snowflakes as established when chart is complete and decreasing 1 st each end on rows indicated on chart, then every ¾ (¾–1–1–1¼–1¼–1¼) inches 6 (8–8–9–9–9–10) times to leave 27 (27–29–33–35–37–39) sts. Then, at 6 (8–9–10–11–12–13) inches from beg, dec 5 (5–5–7–7–7–7) sts evenly in row to leave 22 (22–24–26–28–30–32) sts. With size 3 needles, work in k 1, p 1 rib for 1½ (1½–2–2–2–2–2) inches. Bind off all sts in rib.

FINISHING: Sew underarm and side seams. Sew buttons on left shoulder extension.

KNITTED BY KATHY BAKER

A
B
C

MOOSE PULLOVER CHART 1

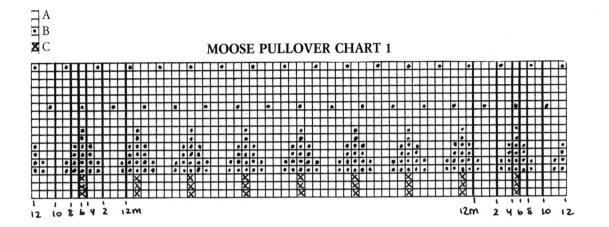

12 10 8 6 4 2 12m   12m 2 4 6 8 10 12

MOOSE PULLOVER CHART 2

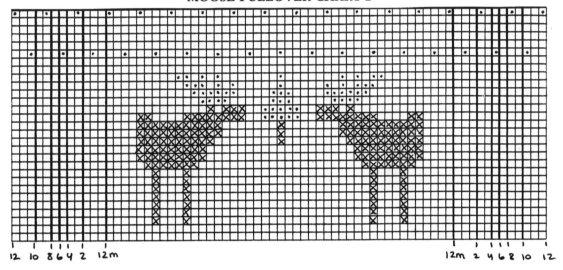

12 10 8 6 4 2 12m   12m 2 4 6 8 10 12

MOOSE PULLOVER CHART 3

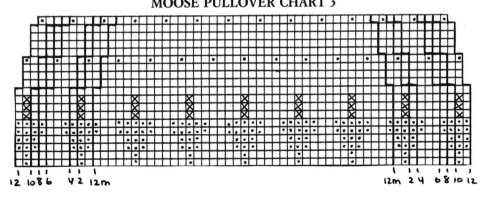

12 10 8 6   4 2 12m   12m 2 4   6 8 10 12

Moose Cardigan

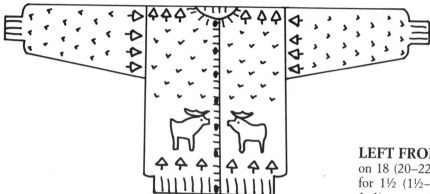

SIZES: Instructions are for size 2. Changes for sizes 4, 6, 8, 10, and 12 are in parentheses. Finished chest measurements are 23¼ (25½–26¾–27¾–29–31¼) inches.

MATERIALS: 7 (9–10–11–13–15) oz or 245 (315–350–385–445–510) yds bulky weight Maine wool for main color (MC); 50 yards each Bartlett-yarns Natural White and Light Sheep's Grey; 25 yards contrasting color (CC). 1 pair each size 8 and size 10 needles or size needed to obtain gauge. 6 (6–6–7–7–7) ¾-inch buttons.

GAUGE: 3.5 sts = 1 inch.

BACK: With size 8 needles and MC, cast on 38 (42–44–46–48–52) sts. Work in k 1, p 1 rib for 1½ (1½–1¾–1¾–2–2) inches, inc 1 st in last row to make 39 (43–45–47–49–53) sts. Then, with size 10 needles, work in stockinette stitch (k 1 row, p 1 row) for 3 rows. With wrong side facing, work Chart 1 for 5 rows. Then work Chart 2, continuing snowflakes as established when Chart 2 is complete. At 8 (9½–10½–11–11½–12) inches from beginning, place markers at each end of needle for armhole. Continue as established until 3 (3½–3¾–4–4½–5) inches above markers. Work Chart 1 for 5 rows. Then, with MC, work even until 4½ (5–5¼–5½–6–6½) inches above markers.

SHAPE SHOULDERS: Bind off 13 (15–15–16–16–18) sts. Leave next 13 (13–15–15–17–17) sts on holder for back of neck. Bind off remaining sts.

LEFT FRONT: With size 8 needles and MC, cast on 18 (20–22–22–24–26) sts. Work in k 1, p 1 rib for 1½ (1½–1¾–1¾–2–2) inches. Inc 2 (2–1–2–1–1) sts evenly in last row to make 20 (22–23–24–25–27) sts. Change to size 10 needles. Then, in stockinette stitch, work Charts 1 and 2 at lower edge and Chart 1 at top edge the same as for the back. At the same time, at 2½ (3–3¼–3½–4–4½) inches above armhole markers, begin neck opening.

SHAPE NECK: At center edge, leave 4 (4–5–5–6–6) sts on holder for front of neck, then dec 1 st at same edge every other row 3 times to make 13 (15–15–16–16–18) sts. Work even until front is same length as back from underarm to shoulder. Bind off all sts.

RIGHT FRONT: Work as for left front, reversing charts and shaping.

SLEEVES: Sew shoulder seams. With size 10 needles and MC, pick up and k 31 (35–37–39–43–45) sts between markers. Purl back. Work in stockinette stitch for 1 row. Then, with wrong side facing, work Chart 3, continuing snowflakes as established and decreasing 1 st each end as indicated on chart, then decreasing again every 1¼ (1¼–1–1¼–1¼–1¼) inches 5 (6–7–7–8–8) times more to leave 19 (21–21–23–25–27) sts. Work even until 8 (9½–10¼–11¼–12–13) inches from beginning, decreasing 3 (3–3–1–3–3) sts evenly in last row to leave 16 (18–18–22–22–24) sts. With size 8 needles, work in k 1, p 1 rib for 1½ (1½–1¾–1¾–2–2) inches. Bind off all sts loosely in rib.

KNITTED BY JOANNE HUTCHINSON

NECK BAND: With right side facing, using size 8 needles and MC, work across 4 (4–5–5–6–6) sts from front holder, pick up and k 11 sts on side of neck, work across 13 (13–15–15–17–17) sts from back holder, pick up and k 11 sts on side of neck, work across 4 (4–5–5–6–6) sts from front holder. Work on these 43 (43–47–47–51–51) sts in k 1, p 1 rib for 1 inch. Bind off all sts in rib.

BUTTONHOLE BAND: With right side facing, using size 10 needles and MC, pick up and k 41

(47–51–55–57–61) sts on left side for girl, right side for boy, and work k 1, p 1 rib for 1 inch. Bind off all sts. Work in same manner on opposite side for ½ inch. Then, evenly space 6 (6–6–7–7–7) one-stitch buttonholes (see Special Techniques chapter) in band, having first and last buttonholes ½ inch from top and bottom edges. Work for ½ inch more. Bind off all sts in rib.

FINISHING: Sew underarm and side seams. Sew buttons.

MOOSE CARDIGAN CHART 1

☐ MAIN COLOR
⊡ NATURAL WHITE
☒ LIGHT SHEEP'S GREY
■ CONTRAST COLOR

work to and from here for front

MOOSE CARDIGAN CHART 2

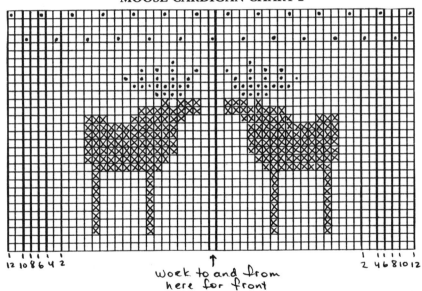

work to and from here for front

MOOSE CARDIGAN CHART 3

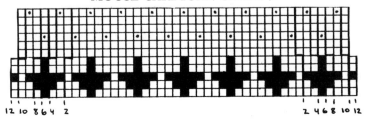

Deer Pullover

SIZES: Instructions are for size 2. Changes for sizes 4, 6, 8, 10, and 12 are in parentheses. Finished chest measurements are 22½ (24–25½–26½–28–30½) inches.

MATERIALS: 7 (8–9–11–12–14) oz or 370 (420–475–580–630–735) yds worsted weight Maine wool for main color (MC); 1 oz or 50 yds each (all sizes) Bartlettyarns Dark Sheep's Grey, Light Sheep's Grey, and green; 10 yards red. 1 pair each size 3 and size 4 needles, or size needed to obtain gauge. 3 ½-inch buttons. 1 tapestry needle.

GAUGE: 5 sts = 1 inch.

BACK: With size 3 needles and MC, cast on 54 (58–62–64–68–74) sts. Work in k 1, p 1 rib for 1 (1½–1½–1½–2–2) inches, inc 2 sts evenly in last row to make 56 (60–64–66–70–76) sts. Then, with size 4 needles, work even in stockinette stitch (k 1 row, p 1 row) until 8 (9½–10–10½–11–11½) inches from beg.

SHAPE ARMHOLE: Bind off 3 sts at beg of next 2 rows, then dec 1 st each end of every other row 3 times to make 44 (48–52–54–58–64) sts. Work even until 4¾ (5–5¼–5½–6–6½) inches above armhole.

SHAPE SHOULDER: With right side facing, bind off 12 (14–15–16–17–20) sts at beg of next row, leave next 20 (20–22–22–24–24) sts on holder for back of neck, work in k 1, p 1 rib on remaining sts for 1 inch more for shoulder extension.

FRONT: Work as for back until lower ribbing is complete. Work 4 rows of stockinette stitch with MC. Then work chart. At the same time, shape armhole at 8 (9½–10–10½–11–11½) inches from beg and work even until 3 (3½–3½–3½–4–4½) inches above armhole.

SHAPE LEFT SHOULDER: On the next right-side row, work across 14 (16–17–18–19–22) sts. Leave remaining sts on holder. Then, dec 1 st at neck edge every other row 2 times to leave 12 (14–15–16–17–20) sts. Work even until 4 (4¼–4½–4¾–5¼–5¾) inches above armhole. Work in k 1, p 1 rib for ¼ inch.

WORK TWO BUTTONHOLES: With right side facing, work 2 (4–5–6–7–10) sts in ribbing, k 2 tog, yo, work 3 sts, k 2 tog, yo, work 3 sts. Continue as established until ribbing is ¾ inch wide. Bind off all sts.

RIGHT SHOULDER: Leave center 16 (16–18–18–20–20) sts on holder for neck. Work on remaining sts in stockinette stitch, dec 1 st at neck edge every other row 2 times. Work even until 4¾ (5–5¼–5½–6–6½) inches above armhole. Bind off all sts.

SLEEVES: With size 3 needles and MC, cast on 28 (30–32–34–36–38) sts. Work in k 1, p 1 rib for 1½ (1½–1½–1½–2–2) inches, inc 6 (5–5–4–5–5) sts evenly in last row to make 34 (35–37–38–41–43) sts. Then, with size 4 needles, work in stockinette stitch, inc 1 st at each end every 1¾ inches 2 (4–4–5–6–6) times to make 38 (43–45–48–53–55) sts. Work even until sleeve measures 9½ (11–12–13–14–15) inches from beg.

KNITTED BY THEO HEALD

SHAPE ARMHOLE AND CAP: Bind off 3 sts at beg of next 2 rows, then 1 st at each end of every other row until 16 (19–19–20–25–25) sts remain. Then bind off 3 (4–4–4–3–3) sts at beg of next 4 (4–4–4–6–6) rows. Bind off remaining 4 (3–3–4–7–7) sts.

NECK BAND: Sew right shoulder seam. With right side facing and using size 3 needles, pick up and k 13 (13–14–15–15–15) sts on left side of neck, work across 16 (16–18–18–20–20) sts from front holder, pick up and k 13 (13–14–15–15–15) sts on right side of neck, work across 20 (20–22–22–24–24) sts from back holder, pick up and k 5 sts on shoulder extension. Work on these 67 (67–73–75–79–79) sts in k 1, p 1 rib for ¼ inch. On next right-side row, work 2 sts, make 1 one-stitch buttonhole as on shoulder, work across as established. Work even until band is ¾ inch wide. Bind off all sts in rib.

FINISHING: Overlap left front shoulder on left back shoulder extension and pin in place. Set in sleeves at shoulder. Sew underarm and side seams. Sew buttons on shoulder extension. Work French Knots as indicated on chart. (Instructions for French Knots can be found in Special Techniques chapter.)

DEER PULLOVER CHART

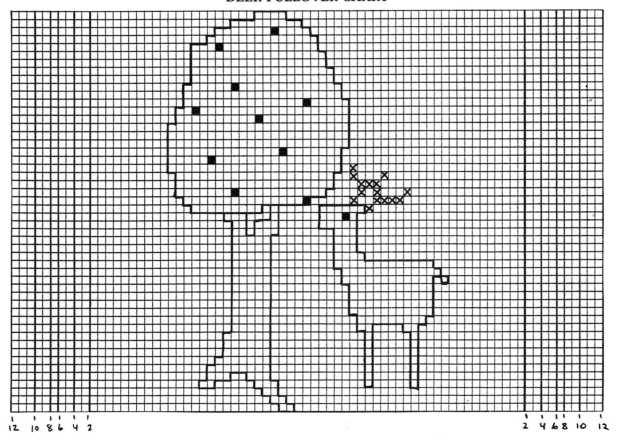

DEER BODY: LIGHT SHEEP'S GREY
ANTLER: DARK SHEEP'S GREY
TREE TRUNK: DARK SHEEP'S GREY
TREE LEAVES: GREEN
APPLES: RED—FRENCH KNOTS
DEER'S EYE: DARK SHEEP'S GREY—FRENCH KNOTS

Puffin Pullover

SIZES: Instructions are for size 2. Changes for sizes 4, 6, 8, 10, and 12 are in parentheses. Finished chest measurements are 22 (24¼–25–26–28–30¼) inches.

MATERIALS: 6 (8–9–10–11–12) oz or 330 (405–450–515–590–665) yds worsted weight washable wool for main color (MC); 2 (2–2–3–3–3) oz or 90 (110–120–140–160–180) yds white; 1 (1–2–2–2–2) yds or 45 (55–60–70–80–90) yds black; 25 yards of orange. 1 pair each size 3 and size 5 needles or size needed to obtain gauge. 1 crochet hook size F, 4 ½-inch buttons, 1 tapestry needle.

GAUGE: 5.5 sts = 1 inch.

BACK: With size 3 needles and MC, cast on 58 (64–66–68–74–80) sts. Work in k 1, p 1 rib for 1½ inches, inc 3 sts evenly in last row to make 61 (67–69–71–77–83) sts. Change to size 5 needles. Then, in stockinette stitch (k 1 row, p 1 row), work Chart 1, continuing pattern until 8 (9½–10–10½–11–11½) inches from beg, or desired length to underarm. Place markers at both ends of needle for armhole. Work for ¼ (½–¾–1–1½–2) inch more. Work 2 rows with MC only. Then, work 22 rows of Chart 2 as follows: MC on 4 (7–8–2–5–1) sts, Chart 2, then MC on 3 sts. Repeat Chart 2 plus 3 MC sts sequence 3 (3–3–4–4–5) times. End with Chart 2, then MC on 4 (7–8–2–5–1) sts. You will have 4 (4–4–5–5–6) puffins across. When puffins chart is complete, work in garter stitch (k every row) until 4¾ (5–5¼–5½–6–6½) inches above armhole markers.

SHAPE NECK: In garter stitch, work across 15 (18–18–19–21–24) sts, bind off next 31 (31–33–33–35–35) sts, work to end of row in garter st. Then, using two balls of yarn and working both sides at the same time, work even for 1 inch on both sides of neck opening. Bind off all sts.

FRONT: Work as for back until 4¾ (5–5¼–5½–6–6½) inches above armhole. Next row, bind off 15 (18–18–19–21–24) sts, place marker for neck opening, bind off 31 (31–33–33–35–35) sts, place marker, bind off remaining sts.

SLEEVES: With size 3 needles and MC, cast on 28 (30–32–34–38–40) sts. Work in k 1, p 1 rib for 1½ inches. Inc 5 sts evenly in last row to make 33 (35–37–39–43–45) sts. Change to size 5 needles. Then, in stockinette stitch work Chart 3, continuing pattern as established, inc 1 st each side as indicated on chart, then every ¾ inch 9 (9–9–10–11–12) times more to make 53 (55–57–61–67–71) sts. Work even until 10 (11–12–13–14–15) inches from beg, or desired length to underarm. Bind off all sts loosely.

FINISHING: With crochet hook and MC, work 1 row single crochet on top edge of front, evenly spacing 2 chain-3 buttonloops on each side of neck markers, having buttonloop closest to center ½ inch from neck opening (See Special Techniques chapter for crochet instructions). Overlap front over back shoulder extensions and sew sleeves at shoulder between markers. Sew underarm and side seams. Sew buttons. With tapestry needle and black yarn, work 1 French Knot for puffins' eyes, as indicated on chart. (Instructions for French Knots can be found in Special Techniques chapter.)

KNITTED BY THEO HEALD

PUFFIN PULLOVER CHART 1

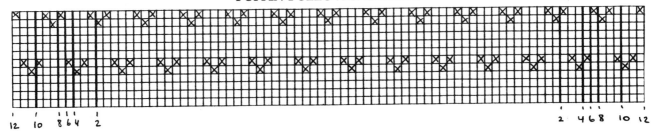

12 10 8 6 4   2   2 4 6 8 10 12

PUFFIN PULLOVER CHART 2

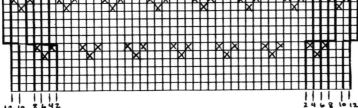

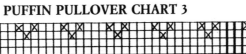

☐ MAIN COLOR
☒ WHITE
◪ BLACK
⊡ ORANGE

PUFFIN PULLOVER CHART 3

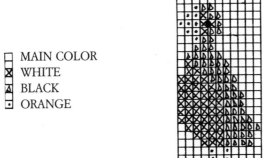

12 10 8 6 4 2   2 4 6 8 10 12

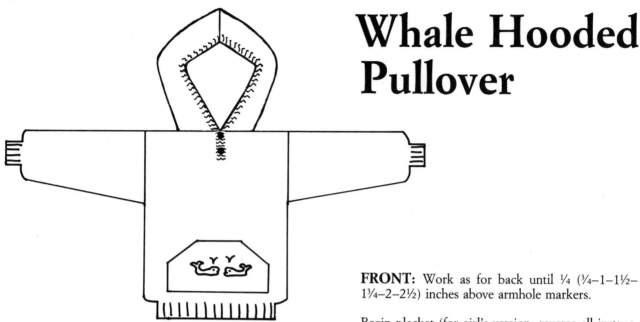

Whale Hooded Pullover

SIZES: Instructions are for size 12 months. Changes for sizes 2, 4, 6, 8, 10, and 12 are in parentheses. Finished chest measurements are 20 (22½–24¼–25¼–26¼–28–30½) inches.

MATERIALS: 8 (10–13–15–16–18–20) oz or 400 (515–625–725–805–895–1015) yds worsted weight Maine wool for main color (MC); 1 oz or 50 yds (all sizes) for contrasting color (CC). Scraps of another color for whales' eyes. 1 pair each size 3 and size 5 needles, or size needed to obtain gauge, 1 size 5 circular needle, 1 size F crochet hook, 2 ½-inch buttons.

GAUGE: 4.5 sts = 1 inch.

BACK: With size 3 needles and MC, cast on 44 (50–54–56–58–62–68) sts. Work in k 1, p 1 rib for 1 (1½–1½–1¾–1¾–2–2) inches, inc 1 st in last row to make 45 (51–55–57–59–63–69) sts. Then, with size 5 needles, work in stockinette stitch (k 1 row, p 1 row) until 7½ (8–9½–10–10½–11–11½) inches from beg. Place markers at both ends of needle for armhole. Continue as established until 4¼ (4¾–5–5½–5¾–6–6½) inches above armhole markers.

SHAPE SHOULDER: Bind off 14 (17–18–19–20–21–24) sts at beg of next row, leave next 17 (17–19–19–19–21–21) sts on holder, bind off remaining sts.

FRONT: Work as for back until ¼ (¾–1–1½–1¾–2–2½) inches above armhole markers.

Begin placket (for girl's version; reverse all instructions for boy's): Next right-side row, work across 20 (23–25–26–27–29–32) sts, leave next 25 (28–30–31–32–34–37) sts on holder. Turn. Cast on 5 sts at beg of next wrong-side row, work in garter stitch (k every row) on these 5 sts to form the placket. On the other sts work as established to end of row. Continue in this manner for 2 inches.

SHAPE NECK: Leave 7 (7–8–8–8–9–9) sts at neck edge on holder, then dec 1 st at same edge every other row 4 times to leave 14 (17–18–19–20–21–24) sts. Work even until same length to shoulder as back. Bind off all sts. Work across first 5 sts from holder in garter stitch for other half of placket, then to end of row as established. Complete this side as for first side, reversing shaping and working first one-stitch buttonhole in center of placket band ½ inch above start of band and second buttonhole 1 inch higher. (See Special Techniques chapter for instructions on how to make a one-stitch buttonhole.)

SLEEVES: Sew shoulder seams. With right side facing, using size 5 needles and MC, pick up and k 39 (43–45–51–53–55–59) sts on armhole edge between markers. Purl back. Work in stockinette stitch, dec 1 st at each end every ¾ (¾–¾–¾–1–1–1) inches 7 (9–9–10–10–10–11) times to leave 25 (25–27–31–33–35–37) sts. Then, at 6 (8–9–10–11–12–13)

KNITTED BY SUSAN DARNEILLE

inches from beg, dec 1 (1–1–3–3–3–3) sts evenly in last row to leave 24 (24–26–28–30–32–34) sts. With size 3 needles, work in k 1, p 1 rib until sleeve measures 7½ (9½–11–12–13–14–15) inches from beg. Bind off all sts loosely in rib.

HOOD: With right side facing, using size 5 circular needle and MC, begin at right front and work across 7 (7–8–8–8–9–9) sts from holder, pick up and k 15 sts on side of neck, work across 17 (17–19–19–19–21–21) sts from back holder, pick up and k 15 sts of side of neck, work across 7 (7–8–8–8–9–9) sts from front holder. Work back and forth on these 61 (61–65–65–65–69–69) sts in stockinette stitch, keeping first and last 5 sts in garter stitch. Work even until 9 (9–9½–10–10½–11–11) inches from beg. Bind off all sts.

POCKET: With size 5 needles and MC, cast on 33 (33–33–35–35–35–39) sts and work in stockinette stitch for ½ (½–½–1–1–1½–1½) inches. Work chart, and at the same time, at 2 (2–2–2½–2½–3–3) inches from beg, shape sides: Dec 1 st each end of every other row until 13 sts remain. Bind off all sts. Work duplicate stitches for whales' eyes (instructions for duplicate stitch in Special Techniques chapter).

FINISHING: Sew underarm and side seams. Overlap inside and outside plackets at neck and slip-stitch bottom edge of inside one in place. Sew buttons opposite buttonholes. With crochet hook and CC, work 1 row single crochet around edge of pocket. Pin pocket in place. Sew top, bottom, and side edges to front, leaving diagonal edges open for hands.

WHALE PULLOVER CHART

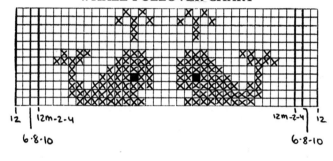

☐ MAIN COLOR
☒ CONTRAST COLOR
■ COLOR FOR EYES—DUPLICATE STITCH

Lighthouse Pullover

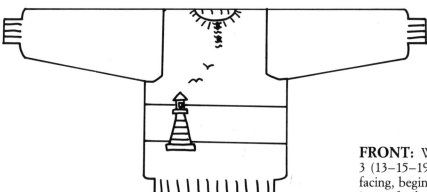

SIZES: Instructions are for size 2. Changes for sizes 4, 6, 8, 10, and 12 are in parentheses. Finished chest measurements are 22 (24¼–25–26–28–30¼) inches.

MATERIALS: 5 (6–7–8–9–10) oz or 275 (325–365–415–480–535) yds light blue worsted weight washable wool; 1 (2–2–3–3–4) oz or 55 (100–115–130–155–180) yds green; 2 oz or 90 yds (all sizes) dark blue; 10 yds each white, red, black and yellow. 1 pair each size 3 and size 5 needles or size needed to obtain gauge. 1 size 3 16-inch circular needle, 2 (2–2–3–3–3) ½-inch buttons.

GAUGE: 5.5 sts = 1 inch, 7 rows = 1 inch.

BACK: With size 3 needles and green yarn, cast on 58 (64–66–68–74–80) sts. Work in k 1, p 1 rib for 1½ inches, inc 3 sts evenly in last row to make 61 (67–69–71–77–83) sts. Then, with size 5 needles, work in stockinette stitch (k 1 row, p 1 row) for 8 (18–20–24–28–32) rows. (*Note:* Size 2 has a relatively narrow green band at lower edge because it is 1½ inches shorter than the next size.) Next, with dark blue, work exactly 21 rows. Continue with light blue until 8 (9½–10–10½–11–11½) inches from beg, or desired length to underarm.

SHAPE ARMHOLE: Bind off 4 sts at beg of next 2 rows, then dec 1 st each end of every other row 3 times to leave 47 (53–55–57–63–69) sts. Work even until 4¾ (5–5¼–5½–6–6½) inches above armhole.

SHAPE SHOULDER: Bind off 13 (16–16–17–19–22) sts, leave next 21 (21–23–23–25–25) sts on holder for back of neck, bind off remaining sts.

FRONT: Work as for back until you have worked 3 (13–15–19–23–27) rows. Then, with wrong side facing, begin working chart, working armhole shaping as for back where required. On next row, once armhole shaping is completed, work across 21 (24–25–26–29–32) sts and leave rest of sts on holder. With wrong side facing, cast on 5 sts at beginning of next row, work these first 5 sts in garter stitch (k every row) for placket and work remaining sts as established. Work in this manner until 2¾ (3–3¼–3½–4–4½) inches above armhole. (*Note:* Directions for placket are given for a girl's pullover and should be reversed if making a boy's pullover).

SHAPE NECK: At neck edge of left front, leave 9 (9–10–10–11–11) sts on holder, then at same edge, dec 1 st every other row 4 times to leave 13 (16–16–17–19–22) sts. When armhole is same depth as on the back, bind off all sts. For right front, work across sts on holder, working first 5 sts in garter st for placket. Complete this side as for left side, reversing shaping and evenly spacing 1 (1–1–2–2–2) one-stitch buttonholes in placket. Allow for the fact that one more buttonhole will be worked in center of neck band. (See Special Techniques chapter for instructions on how to make one-stitch buttonholes.)

SLEEVES: With size 3 needles and light blue yarn, cast on 28 (30–32–34–36–38) sts. Work in k 1, p 1 rib for 1½ inches, inc 5 sts evenly in last row to make 33 (35–37–39–41–43) sts. Work in stockinette stitch with size 5 needles, inc 1 st every 1½ inches 5 (6–6–7–8–8) times to make 43 (47–49–53–57–59) sts.

Work even until 10 (11–12–13–14–15) inches from beg or desired length to underarm.

SHAPE ARMHOLE AND CAP: Bind off 4 sts at beg of next 2 rows, then dec 1 st at each end of every other row until 17 sts remain. Bind off 3 sts at beg of next 4 rows. Bind off remaining 5 sts.

NECK BAND: Sew shoulder seams. Then, with right side facing, using size 3 circular needle and light blue yarn, work across 9 (9–10–10–11–11) sts from front holder, pick up and k 14 sts on right side of neck, work across 21 (21–23–23–25–25) sts from back holder, pick up and k 14 sts on left side of neck, work across 9 (9–10–10–11–11) sts from front holder. Work on these 67 (67–71–71–75–75) sts in k 1, p 1 rib for ¾ inch, working last one-stitch buttonhole at half-way point. Bind off loosely in rib.

FINISHING: Set in sleeves and sew underarm and side seams, matching stripes at sides. Slip-stitch placket edge to inside. Sew buttons opposite buttonholes. Using tapestry needle and white yarn, work duplicate stitch for seagulls, following design on chart. (The Special Techniques chapter includes instructions for duplicate stitch.)

LIGHTHOUSE PULLOVER CHART

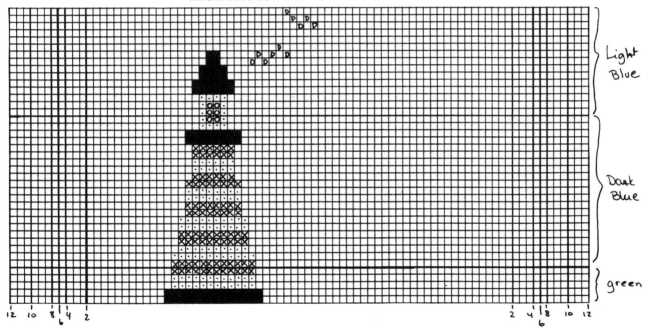

■ BLACK
· WHITE
✕ RED
⊙ YELLOW—EITHER KNITTED OR DUPLICATE STITCH
◨ WHITE—DUPLICATE STITCH

Sailboat Pullover

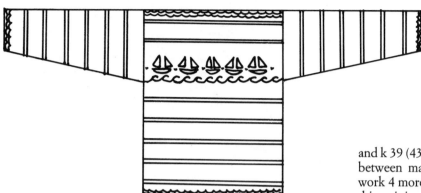

SIZES: Instructions are for size 12 months. Changes for sizes 2, 4, 6, 8, 10, and 12 are in parentheses. Finished chest measurements are 20 (22½–24½–25¼–26¼–28–30½) inches.

MATERIALS: 5 (6–7–8–9–10–12) oz or 265 (315–370–420–475–525–630) yds worsted weight Maine wool for main color (MC); 2 oz or 50 yds (all sizes) for contrasting color (CC). 1 pair each size 3 and size 5 needles or size needed to obtain gauge.

GAUGE: 4.5 sts = 1 inch.

BACK: With size 3 needles and MC, cast on 45 (51–55–57–59–63–69) sts and work in garter stitch (k every row) for 6 rows. Then, with size 5 needles, work in stockinette stitch (k 1 row, p 1 row) as follows: 6 rows MC, 2 rows CC. Work as established until 7½ (8–9½–10–10½–11–11½) inches from beg. Place markers at both ends of needle for armhole. Work chart, then return to stripes pattern when chart is complete and work until 3½ (4–4¼–4¾–5–5¼–5¾) inches above armhole markers. With MC, work in garter stitch for 6 rows. Bind off all sts loosely.

FRONT: Work as for back.

SLEEVES: Sew shoulder seams, leaving a 6½ (6½–7–7–7–7½–7½)-inch neck opening. With right side facing, using size 5 needles and MC, pick up and k 39 (43–45–51–53–55–59) sts on armhole edge between markers. Purl back. In stockinette stitch, work 4 more rows in MC, then 2 rows in CC. Repeat this striping pattern as for back, dec 1 st at each end of row every ¾ (¾–¾–¾–1–1–1) inch 7 (9–9–10–10–10–11) times to leave 25 (25–27–31–33–35–37) sts. Work even until sleeve measures 6 (8–9–10–11–12–13) inches from beg, decreasing 3 (3–3–5–5–5–5) sts evenly in last row to leave 22 (22–24–26–28–30–32) sts. With size 3 needles, work in k 1, p 1 rib for 1½ (1½–2–2–2–2–2) inches for cuff. Bind off all sts in rib.

FINISHING: Sew underarm and side seams.

KNITTED BY KATHY BAKER

☐ MAIN COLOR
☒ CONTRAST COLOR

SAILBOAT PULLOVER CHART

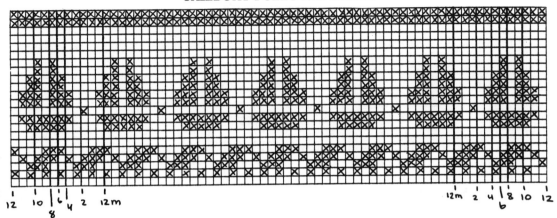

Pine Tree Pullover

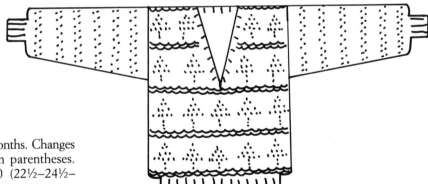

SIZES: Instructions are for size 12 months. Changes for sizes 2, 4, 6, 8, 10, and 12 are in parentheses. Finished chest measurements are 20 (22½–24½–25¼–26¼–28–30½) inches.

MATERIALS: 6 (7–8–9–10–11–13) oz or 280 (340–420–465–505– 565–650) yds worsted weight Maine wool for color A; 2 (2–2–3–3–4–4) oz or 60 (75–95–110–125–135–145) yds for color B. 1 pair each size 3 and size 5 needles or size needed to obtain gauge.

GAUGE: 4.5 sts = 1 inch in stockinette stitch.

PATTERNS USED
Pine tree motif
Rows 1 and 3: K 3A, p 1B, k 3A.
Rows 2 and 4: P 3A, p 1B, p 3A.
Rows 5 and 8: (P 1B, k 1A) 3 times, p 1B.
Rows 6 and 7: (K 1B, p 1A) 3 times, k 1B.

Row 9: K 2A, p 1B, k 1A, p 1B, k 2A.
Row 10: P 2A, k 1B, p 1A, k 1B, p 2A.
Row 11: K 3A, p 1B, k 3A.
Row 12: P 3A, k 1B, p 3A.
Dotted pattern
Row 1: K 1A, k 1B.
Row 2: P 1B over A, p 1A over B.

BACK: With size 3 needles and color A, cast on 44 (50–54–56–58–62–68) sts. Work in k 1, p 1 rib for 1 (1½–1½–1¾–1¾–2–2) inches, inc 1 st in last row to make 45 (51–55–57–59–63–69) sts. Then, with size 5 needles, work in garter stitch (k every row) for 4 rows, stockinette stitch (k 1 row, p 1 row) for 4 rows. Work pattern for 12 rows as follows: Stockinette stitch on 4 (2–4–5–1–3–1) sts, [pine tree motif on 7 sts, stockinette stitch on 3] 4 (4–5–5–5–6–6) times, end pine tree motif on 0 (7–0–0–7–0–7) sts, stockinette stitch on 1 (2–1–2–1–1–0–1) sts. You will have 4 (5–5–5–6–6–7) pine trees across. Then work in stockinette stitch for 4 rows. Repeat these 24 rows for rest of back. At 7½ (8–9½–10–10½–11–11½) inches from beg, place markers at both ends of needle for armhole. Continue working as established until 4¼ (4¾–5–5½–5¾–6–6½) inches above armhole markers.

SHAPE SHOULDER: Bind off 14 (17–18–19–20–21–24) sts at beg of next row, leave next 17 (17–19–19–19–21–21) sts on holder, bind off remaining sts.

FRONT: Work as for back until ready to place armhole markers.

SHAPE NECK: Bind off center st. Attach a second ball of yarn so you can work both sides of upper front at the same time. Continuing pattern as established, dec 1 st at neck edges every ½ inch 8 (8–9–9–9–10–10) times to leave 14 (17–18–19–20–21–24) sts on each side of V-shaped neck opening. Work even until same same length to shoulder as back. Bind off all sts.

NECK BAND: Sew right shoulder seam. With right side facing, using size 3 needles and color A, begin at left shoulder and pick up and k 28 (30–32–33–34–36–38) sts on left side of neck, pick up and k 1 st in center of V, pick up and k 28 (30–32–33–34–36–38) sts on right side of neck, work across 17 (17–19–19–19–21–21) sts from back holder. Work on these 74 (78–84–86–88–94–98) sts in k 1, p 1 rib, dec 1 st on each side of st in center of V every row, until band measures ¾ inch wide (be sure to k st in center of V on the right side and p it on the wrong side). Bind off all sts loosely in rib.

SLEEVES: Sew side of neck band and left shoulder seam. With right side facing, using size 5 needles and color A, pick up and k 39 (43–45–51–53–55–59) sts on armhole edge between markers. Purl back. Work 4 rows stockinette stitch. Then, work stripes pattern for rest of sleeve as follows: In stockinette stitch, work 2 rows dotted pattern, 6 rows color A. At the same time, dec 1 st every ¾ (¾–1–1–1–1¼–1¼) inch 6 (8–8–9–9–9–10) times to leave 27 (27–29–33–35–37–39) sts. Then, at 6 (8–9–10–11–12–13) inches from beg, decrease 3 (3–3–5–5–5–5) sts evenly in last row to leave 24 (24–26–28–30–32–34) sts. With size 3 needles, work in k 1, p 1 rib for 2 inches. Bind off all sts loosely in rib.

FINISHING: Sew underarm and side seams.

KNITTED BY THEO HEALD

Blueberry Cardigan

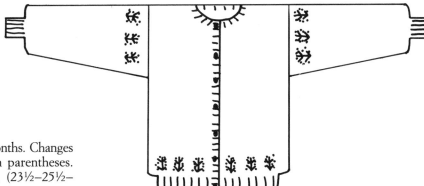

SIZES: Instructions are for size 12 months. Changes for sizes 2, 4, 6, 8, 10, and 12 are in parentheses. Finished chest measurements are 21 (23½–25½–26¼–27¼–29–31½) inches.

MATERIALS: 6 (7–8–9–10–11–13) oz or 315 (365–420–475–525–680–785) yds worsted weight Maine wool for main color (MC); 2 oz or 100 yds (all sizes) color A; 1 oz or 50 yds (all sizes) color B (for blueberries). 1 pair each size 3 and size 5 needles or size needed to obtain gauge. 5 (6–6–6–7–7–7) ½-inch buttons. 1 tapestry needle.

GAUGE: 4.5 sts. = 1 inch.

BACK: With size 3 needles and MC, cast on 44 (50–54–56–58–62–68) sts. Work in k 1, p 1 rib for 1 (1½–1½–1¾–1¾–2–2) inches, inc 1 st in last row to make 45 (51–55–57–59–63–69) sts. Then, with size 5 needles, work in stockinette stitch (k 1 row, p 1 row) for 4 rows. Begin Chart 1, continuing with MC only after chart is complete. At 7½ (8–9½–10–10½–11–11½) inches from beg, place markers at both ends of needle for armhole. Work even until 4¼ (4¾–5–5½–5¾–6–6½) inches above armhole markers.

SHAPE SHOULDER: Bind off 14 (17–18–19–20–21–24) sts at beg of next row, leave next 17 (17–19–19–19–21–21) sts on holder, bind off remaining sts.

FRONT: With size 3 needles and MC, cast on 22 (24–26–28–30–32–34) sts. Work in k 1, p 1 rib for 1 (1½–1½–1¾–1¾–2–2) inches, inc 1 (2–2–1–0–0–1) sts in last row to make 23 (26–28–29–30–32–35) sts. Then, with size 5 needles, work in stockinette stitch for 4 rows. Work Chart 1, continuing with MC as for back until 2½ (2¾–3–3½–3¾–4–4½) inches above armhole markers.

SHAPE NECK: Put 5 (5–6–6–6–7–7) sts on holder at neck edge, then dec 1 st at same edge every other row 4 times to leave 14 (17–18–19–20–21–24) sts. Work even until same length to shoulder as back. Bind off all sts. Work other half of front, reversing neck shaping.

SLEEVES: Sew shoulder seams. With right side facing, using size 5 needles and MC, pick up and k 39 (43–45–51–53–55–59) sts on armhole edge between markers. Purl back. Work 2 rows of stockinette stitch, then work Chart 2. When chart is complete, dec 1 st at each end every ½ (¾–¾–¾–1–1–1) inch 6 (8–8–9–9–9–10) times to leave 27 (27–29–33–35–37–39) sts. Then, at 6 (8–9–10–11–12–13) inches from beg, decrease 3 (3–3–5–5–5–5) sts evenly in last row to leave 24 (24–26–28–30–32–34) sts. With size 3 needles, work in k 1, p 1 rib for 1½ (1½–2–2–2–2–2) inches. Bind off all sts in rib.

NECK BAND: With right side facing, using size 3 needles and MC, work across 5 (5–6–6–6–7–7) sts from front holder, pick up and k 12 sts from one side of neck, work across 17 (17–19–19–19–21–21) sts from back holder, pick up and k 12 sts from other side of neck, work across 5 (5–6–6–6–7–7) sts from front holder. Work on these 51 (51–55–55–55–59

KNITTED BY KATHY BAKER

−59) sts in k 1, p 1 rib for 1 inch. Bind off all sts loosely in rib.

BUTTONHOLE BAND: With right side facing, using size 5 needles and MC, pick up and k 49 (53 −61−65−69−73−77) sts on edge of left front and work in k 1, p 1 rib for 1 inch. Bind off all sts. Work in same manner on edge of right front for ½ inch. Then, evenly space 5 (6−6−6−7−7−7) one-stitch but-

tonholes in band, having first and last buttonholes ½ inch from ends of band. Work for ½ inch more. Bind off all sts in rib.

FINISHING: Sew underarm and side seams. Sew buttons. With tapestry needle and color B, work French Knots for blueberries as indicated on Chart 3. (Instructions for French Knots can be found in Special Techniques chapter.)

BLUEBERRY CARDIGAN CHART 1

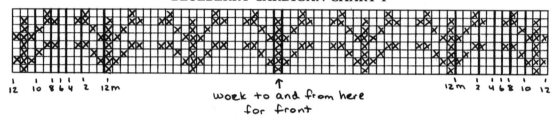

work to and from here for front

BLUEBERRY CARDIGAN CHART 2

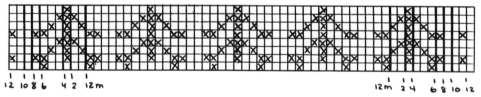

☐ MAIN COLOR
☒ A

BLUEBERRY CARDIGAN CHART 3

Blueberry Vest

SIZES: Instructions are for size 12 months. Changes for sizes 2, 4, 6, 8, 10, and 12 are in parentheses. Finished chest measurements are 20 (22½–24½–25¼–26¼–28–30½) inches.

MATERIALS: 4 (4–5–6–6–7–8) oz or 165 (200–250–275–300–335–385) yds worsted weight Maine wool for main color (MC); 2 oz or 100 yds (all sizes) color A; 1 oz or 50 yds (all sizes) color B (for blueberries). 1 pair each size 3 and size 5 needles or size needed to obtain gauge. 1 tapestry needle.

GAUGE: 4.5 sts. = 1 inch.

BACK: With size 3 needles and MC, cast on 44 (50–54–56–58–62–68) sts. Work in k 1, p 1 rib for 1 (1½–1½–1¾–1¾–2–2) inches, inc 1 st in last row to make 45 (51–55–57–59–63–69) sts. Then, with size 5 needles, work in stockinette stitch (k 1 row, p 1 row) for 4 rows. Begin Chart 1, repeating these 24 rows until 7 (7½–9–9½–10–10½–11) inches from beg. Place markers at both ends of needle for armhole. Continue working chart as established until 4¾ (5¼–5½–6–6¼–6½–7) inches above armhole markers.

SHAPE SHOULDER: Bind off 14 (17–18–19–20–21–24) sts at beg of next row, leave next 17 (17–19–19–19–21–21) sts on holder, bind off remaining sts.

FRONT: Work as for back until ready to place armhole markers. Shape neck: Bind off center st. Attach second ball of yarn so you can work both sides at the same time. Continuing chart as estab-

BLUEBERRY VEST CHART 1

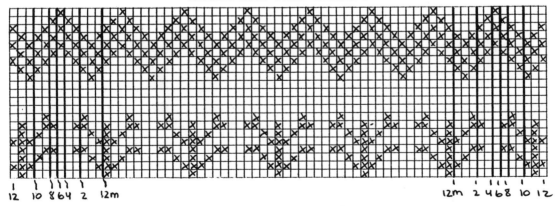

☐ MAIN COLOR
☒ A

BLUEBERRY VEST CHART 2

lished, dec 1 st at neck edge every ½ inch 8 (8–9–9–9–10–10) times to leave 14 (17–18–19–20–21–24) sts on each side of neck opening. Work even until front measures same length to shoulder as back. Bind off all sts.

NECK BAND: Sew right shoulder seam. With right side facing, using size 3 needles and MC, pick up and k 30 (32–34–35–36–38–40) sts on left side of neck, pick up and k 1 st in center of V, pick up and k 30 (32–34–35–36–38–40) sts on right side of neck, work across 17 (17–19–19–19–21–21) sts from back holder. Work on these 78 (82–88–90–92–98–102) sts in k 1, p 1 rib, dec 1 st on each side of st in center of V every row until band measures ¾ inch wide (be sure to k st in center of V on the right side and p it on the wrong side). Bind off all sts loosely in rib.

ARMHOLE BANDS: Sew side of neck band and left shoulder seam. With right side facing, using size 3 needles and MC, pick up and k 42 (46–48–52–54–56–62) sts on armhole edge between markers. Work in k 1, p 1 rib for ¾ inch. Bind off all sts in rib.

FINISHING: Sew side seams. With tapestry needle and color B, work French Knots for blueberries as indicated on chart, following method explained in Special Techniques chapter.

KNITTED BY KATHY BAKER

Traditional Favorites

Aran Vest

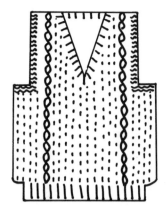

SIZES: Instructions are for size 12 months. Changes for sizes 2, 4, 6, 8, 10, and 12 are in parentheses. Finished chest measurements are 20 (22½–24–25–26½–28–30½) inches.

MATERIALS: 4 (5–6–7–7–8–9) oz or 210 (265–315–365–385–420–470) yds worsted weight Maine wool; 1 pair each sizes 3, 4, and 6 needles or size needed to obtain gauge; 1 double-pointed needle (dpn).

GAUGE: 5 sts = 1 inch in stockinette stitch with size 4 needles.

STITCHES USED
Moss stitch
Row 1: K 1, p 1 across.
Rows 2 and 4: K on k sts, p on p sts across.
Row 3: P 1, k 1 across. Repeat these 4 rows for pattern.
Cable
Row 1: P 2, k 4, p 2.
Row 2 and all even rows: K 2, p 4, k 2.
Row 3: P 2, sl 2 to dpn and hold in front of work, k next 2 sts, k 2 from dpn, p 2.
Rows 5 and 7: same as row 1.
Repeat these 8 rows for cable pattern.
Stockinette stitch (back of vest): K 1 row, p 1 row.

BACK: With size 3 needles, cast on 48 (54–58–60–64–68–74) sts. Work in k 1, p 1 rib for 1¼ (1¼–1½–1½–1¾–1¾–2) inches, inc 2 sts evenly in last row to make 50 (56–60–62–66–70–76) sts. Then, with size 4 needles, work in stockinette stitch until

6½ (7½–9–9½–10–10½–11) inches from beg or ½ inch less than desired length to underarm. Then work 10 (10–10–11–11–12–12) sts in garter stitch (k every row), work across in stockinette stitch to last 10 (10–10–11–11–12–12) sts, work in garter stitch to end of row. Work as established for ½ inch more.

SHAPE ARMHOLE: Bind off 6 (6–6–7–7–8–8) sts at beg of next 2 rows. Continue on remaining 38 (44–48–48–52–54–60) sts as established until 4 (4½–5–5¼–5½–6–6½) inches above armhole.

SHAPE SHOULDER: Bind off 10 (12–14–14–15–16–18) sts at beg of next right-side row, leave next 18 (20–20–20–22–22–24) sts on holder for back of neck, bind off remaining sts.

FRONT: Work as for back until bottom ribbing is complete. Then, with size 6 needles, work 9 (10–11–11–12–13–15) sts in moss stitch, cable on 8 sts, 16 (20–22–24–26–28–30) sts in moss stitch, cable on 8 sts, 9 (10–11–11–12–13–15) sts in moss stitch. Continue as established, beginning to work garter stitch at armhole at same place as on back.

SHAPE NECK: Shape armhole as for back and at the same time shape neck. Divide work evenly in two, and attach another ball of yarn. Working both sides at the same time, dec 1 st at neck edge every ⅓ inch 9 (10–10–10–11–11–12) times to leave 10 (12–14–14–15–16–18) sts. Bind off all sts when armhole is same depth to shoulder as on back.

NECK BAND: Sew right shoulder seam. With right side facing and using size 3 needles, pick up and k 30 (33–35–36–37–40–42) sts on left side of neck, pick up 1 st in center of V, pick up and k 30 (33–35–36–37–40–42) sts on right side of neck, work across 18 (20–20–20–22–22–24) sts from back holder. Work on these 79 (87–91–93–97–103–109) sts in k 1, p 1 rib, dec 1 st on each side of st in center of V every row until band measures ¾ inch wide. (Be sure to k st in center of V on the right side and p it on the wrong side.) Bind off all sts loosely in rib.

FINISHING: Sew left side of neck band and left shoulder seam. Sew side seams.

KNITTED BY LANA BRADBURY

Aran Cardigan

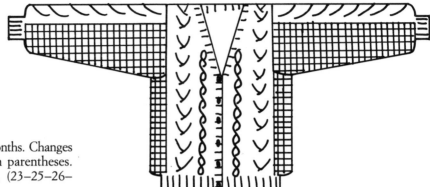

SIZES: Instructions are for size 12 months. Changes for sizes 2, 4, 6, 8, 10, and 12 are in parentheses. Finished chest measurements are 21 (23–25–26–27–29–31) inches.

MATERIALS: 7 (9–11–12–13–15–18) oz or 245 (315–400–445–500–570–655) yds bulky weight Maine wool; 1 pair each size 8 and size 10 needles or size needed to obtain gauge; 1 double-pointed needle (dpn); 4 (5–5–5–5–6–6) ¾-inch buttons.

GAUGE: 3.5 sts = 1 inch in stockinette stitch.

STITCHES USED
Double seed stitch
Row 1: K 2, p 2.
Rows 2 and 4: K on p, p on k.
Row 3: P 2, k 2. Repeat these 4 rows for pattern.
Crossed cable
Row 1: P 4, sl 2 to dpn and hold in back of work, k 2, k 2 from dpn, p 4.
Row 2: K 4, p 4, k 4.
Row 3: P 3, sl 1 to dpn and hold in back of work, k 2, k 1 from dpn (called back cross, or BC); sl 2 to dpn and hold in front of work, k 1, k 2 from dpn (called front cross, or FC), p 3.
Row 4: K 3, p 6, k 3.
Row 5: P 2, BC, k 2, FC, p 2.
Row 6: K 2, p 8, k 2.
Row 7: P 1, BC, k 4, FC, p 1.
Row 8: K 1, p 10, k 1. Repeat these 8 rows for pattern.
Double cable
Rows 1 and 3: P 1, k 4, p 2, k 4, p 1.
Rows 2, 4, and 6: K 1, p 4, k 2, p 4, k 1.
Row 5: P 1, sl 2 to dpn and hold in front of work, k 2, k 2 from dpn, p 2, sl 2 to dpn and hold in front of work, k 2, k 2 from dpn, p 1.
Repeat these 6 rows for pattern.

KNITTED BY THERESA TIMMONS

Single cable
Rows 1 and 3: P 1, k 4, p 2.
Rows 2, 4, and 6: K 2, p 4, p 1.
Row 5: P 1, sl 2 to dpn and hold in front of work, k 2, k 2 from dpn, p 2.

BACK: With size 8 needles, cast on 36 (38–42–44–46–50–54) sts. Work in k 1, p 1 rib for 1 (1½–1½–1¾–1¾–2–2) inches, inc 6 (8–8–8–8–8–8) sts evenly in last row to make 42 (46–50–52–54–58–62) sts. Then, with size 10 needles, work in double seed stitch on 3 (5–7–8–9–11–13) sts, crossed cable on 12 sts, double cable on 12 sts, crossed cable on 12 sts, double seed stitch on 3 (5–7–8–9–11–13) sts. Work as established until 7 (8–9½–10–10½–11–11½) inches from beg.

SHAPE ARMHOLE: Bind off 2 (2–3–3–3–3–3) sts at beg of next 2 rows, then dec 1 st at each end of every other row 2 (2–2–2–2–3–3) times to leave 34 (38–40–42–44–46–50) sts. Work even until 4 (4½–5–5¼–5½–6–6½) inches above armhole.

SHAPE SHOULDER: Bind off 5 (6–6–6–7–7–8) sts at beg of next 2 rows, then 6 (6–7–7–7–7–8) sts at beg of next 2 rows. Leave remaining 12 (14–14–16–16–18–18) sts on holder for back of neck.

FRONT (left): With size 8 needles, cast on 18 (20–22–22–24–26–28) sts. Work in k 1, p 1 rib for 1 (1½–1½–1¾–1¾–2–2) inches, inc 2 (2–2–3–2–2–2) sts evenly in last row to make 20 (22–24–25–26–28–30) sts. Then, with size 10 needles, work in double seed stitch on 1 (3–5–6–7–9–11) sts, crossed cable on 12 sts, single cable on 7 sts. Work as established to armhole.

SHAPE ARMHOLE AND NECK: Shape armhole as for back, and at the same time, shape neck. At neck edge, dec 1 st every ½ inch 5 (6–6–7–7–8–8) times to leave 11 (12–13–13–14–14–16) sts. Work even until armhole is same depth as back to shoulder.

SHAPE SHOULDER: As for back. Work right side in same manner, reversing shaping.

SLEEVES: With size 8 needles, cast on 14 (16–18–18–20–22–24) sts. Work in k 1, p 1 rib for 1 (1½–1½–1¾–1¾–2–2) inches, inc 4 sts evenly in last row to make 18 (20–22–22–24–26–28) sts. Then, with size 10 needles, work in double seed stitch on 3 (4–5–5–6–7–8) sts, crossed cable stitch on 12 sts, double seed stitch to end of row. Work as established, inc 1 st at each end of every 1¼ inches 5 (6–7–8–8–9–9) times to make 28 (32–36–38–40–44–46) sts, working inc sts in double seed stitch. Work even until sleeve measures 7½ (9½–11–12–13–14–15) inches from beg.

SHAPE ARMHOLE AND CAP: Bind off 2 (2–3–3–3–3–3) sts at beg of next 2 rows, then dec 1 st each end of every other row until 16 sts remain. Bind off 2 sts at beg of next 6 rows. Bind off remaining 4 sts.

NECK & BUTTONHOLE BAND: Sew shoulder seams. With right side facing and using size 10 needles (on left side for girls, right side for boys), pick up and k 24 (28–33–35–36–39–41) sts from lower edge to point where neck shaping begins, then 20 (23–24–25–26–28–30) sts along neck edge. Then work across 6 (7–7–8–8–9–9) sts from back holder, leaving remaining sts on holder. Work on these 50 (58–64–68–70–76–80) sts in k 1, p 1 rib for 1 inch. Bind off all sts in rib. Work in same manner on opposite side for ½ inch. Then work buttonholes as follows: Work 1 (2–2–1–2–2–1) sts, [k 2 tog, yo, work on 5 (4–5–6–6–5–6) sts] 3 (4–4–4–4–5–5) times, k 2 tog, yo, work in established ribbing to end of row. Work until band is 1 inch wide. Bind off all sts in rib.

FINISHING: Sew neck band ends together at center back. Set in sleeves at shoulder. Sew underarm and side seams. Sew buttons.

Aran Pullover

SIZES: Instructions are for size 12 months. Changes for sizes 2, 4, 6, 8, 10, and 12 are in parentheses. Finished chest measurements are 20 (22–24–25–26–28–30) inches.

MATERIALS: 7 (9–11–12–13–14–16) oz or 235 (295–370–405–440–505–575) yds bulky weight Maine wool; 1 pair each size 8 and size 10 needles or size needed to obtain gauge; 1 double-pointed needle (dpn).

GAUGE: 3.5 sts = 1 inch in stockinette stitch.

STITCHES USED

Seed stitch
Row 1 (wrong side): K 1, p 1.
Row 2: K on p, p on k.
Repeat these 2 rows for pattern.

Twin ribs
Row 1 (wrong side): K 2, (p 2, k 2) 2 times.
Row 2: P 2, (k 2 tog, leave on left needle, then insert right needle between the 2 sts and k the first st again, drop both sts off left needle together, p 2) 2 times.
Repeat these 2 rows for pattern.

Diamond panel
Row 1 (wrong side): K 4, p 1, k 1, p 1, k 4.
Row 2: P 4, sl next 2 sts to dpn and hold in front of work, sl 1 as if to p, then sl the purl st from dpn to left-hand needle and purl it, then sl other st from dpn as if to p, p 4.
Row 3: Same as row 1.
Row 4: P 3; sl next st to dpn and hold in back of work, sl 1 as if to p, p 1 from dpn (called back cross, or BC); k 1; sl next st to dpn and hold in front of work, p 1, then sl 1 from dpn as if to p (called front cross, or FC); p 3.

Row 5 and all subsequent wrong-side rows: K all k sts, p all p and slipped sts from previous row.
Row 6: P 2, BC, k 1, p 1, k 1, FC, p 2.
Row 8: P 1, BC, (k 1, p 1) 2 times, k 1, FC, p 1.
Row 10: P 1, FC, (p 1, k 1) 2 times, p 1, BC, p 1.
Row 12: P 2, FC, k 1, p 1, k 1, BC, p 2.
Row 14: P 3, FC, k 1, BC, p 3.
Repeat these 14 rows for pattern.

BACK: With size 8 needles, cast on 36 (38–42–44–46–50–54) sts. Work in k 1, p 1 rib for 1 (1½–1½–1¾–1¾–2–2) inches, inc 5 (7–7–7–7–7–7) sts evenly in last row to make 41 (45–49–51–53–57–61) sts. Then, with size 10 needles and wrong side facing, work in seed stitch on 5 (7–9–10–11–13–15) sts, twin ribs on 10 sts, diamond panel on 11 sts, twin ribs on 10 sts, seed stitch on 5 (7–9–10–11–13–15) sts. Work as established until 7 (8–9½–10–10½–11–11½) inches from beg.

SHAPE ARMHOLE: Bind off 2 (2–3–3–3–3–3) sts at beg of next 2 rows, then dec 1 st each end every other row 2 (2–2–2–2–3–3) times to leave 33 (37–39–41–43–45–49) sts. Work even until 4 (4½–5–5¼–5½–6–6½) inches above armhole.

SHAPE SHOULDER: Bind off 5 (6–6–6–7–7–8) sts at beg of next 2 rows, 6 (6–7–7–7–7–8) sts at beg of next 2 rows. Leave remaining 11 (13–13–15–15–17–17) sts on holder for back of neck.

FRONT: Work as for back until 2½ (3–3–3¼–3½–4–4½) inches above armhole.

SHAPE NECK: Leave center 7 (9–9–11–11–13–13) sts on holder. Then, working both sides at the same time, dec 1 st at neck edges every other row 2 times to leave 11 (12–13–13–14–14–16) sts. Work even until armhole is same depth as back to shoulder. Shape shoulder as for back.

SLEEVES: With size 8 needles, cast on 14 (16–18–18–20–22–24) sts. Work in k 1, p 1 rib for 1 (1½–1½–1¾–1¾–2–2) inches, inc 3 sts evenly in last row to make 17 (19–21–21–23–25–27) sts. Then, with size 10 needles and wrong side facing, work in seed stitch on 3 (4–5–5–6–7–8) sts, diamond panel on 11 sts, seed stitch to end of row. Work as established, inc 1 st at each end every 1¼ inch 5 (6–7–8–8–9–9) times to make 27 (31–35–37–39–43–45) sts, working inc sts in seed stitch. Work even until sleeve measures 7½ (9½–11–12–13–14–15) inches from beg.

SHAPE ARMHOLE AND CAP: Bind off 2 (2–3–3–3–3–3) sts at beg of next 2 rows, then dec 1 st at each end of every other row until 15 sts remain. Bind off 2 sts at beg of next 6 rows. Bind off remaining 3 sts.

NECK BAND: Sew right shoulder seam. With right side facing and using size 8 needles, pick up and k 9 (9–11–11–11–11–11) sts on left side of neck, work across 7 (9–9–11–11–13–13) sts from front holder, pick up and k 9 (9–11–11–11–11–11) sts on right side of neck, work across 11 (13–13–15–15–17–17) sts from back holder. Work on these 36 (40–44–48–48–52–52) sts in k 1, p 1 rib for ¾ inch. Bind off all sts loosely in rib using size 10 needle.

FINISHING: Sew side of neck band and left shoulder seam. Set in sleeves at shoulder. Sew underarm and side seams.

Fair Isle Vest

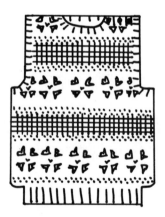

SIZES: Instructions are for size 2. Changes for sizes 4, 6, 8, 10, and 12 are in parentheses. Finished chest measurements are 22¾ (24½–26–27–28½–30¾) inches.

MATERIALS: 4 (5–5–6–6–7) oz or 165 (205–225–245–280–320) yards worsted weight Maine wool for color A; 2 (2–3–3–4–4) oz or 75 (100–125–150–175–200) yds color B; 1 oz or 50 yds (all sizes) color C. 1 pair each size 3 and size 4 needles or size needed to obtain gauge; 3 ½-inch buttons.

GAUGE: 5 sts = 1 inch.

BACK: With size 3 needles and color A, cast on 56 (60–64–66–70–76) sts. Work in k 1, p 1 rib for 1 (1½–1½–1½–2–2) inches, inc 1 st in last row to make 57 (61–65–67–71–77) sts. Then, with size 4 needles, work even in stockinette stitch (k 1 row, p 1 row), following Chart and repeating rows as indicated for rest of piece.

SHAPE ARMHOLE at 7½ (9–9½–10–10½–11) inches from beg. Bind off 3 sts at beg of next 2 rows, then dec 1 st each end every other row 3 times to leave 45 (49–53–55–59–65) sts. Work even until 5 (5½–5¾–6–6½–7) inches above armhole.

SHAPE SHOULDERS: With right side facing, bind off 12 (14–15–16–17–20) sts at beg of next row, leave next 21 (21–23–23–25–25) sts on holder for back of neck, work for 1 inch more in k 1, p 1

KNITTED BY SUSAN DARNEILLE

rib on remaining sts for left shoulder extension. Bind off all sts.

FRONT: Work as for back until 3 (3½–3¾–4–4½–5) inches above armhole.

SHAPE LEFT SHOULDER: On next right side row, work across 14 (16–17–18–19–22) sts, leaving remaining sts on holder. Then, dec 1 st at neck edge every other row 2 times to leave 12 (14–15–16–17–20) sts. Work even until 4 (4½–4¾–5–5½–6) inches above armhole. Work in k 1, p 1 rib for ½ inch.

WORK BUTTONHOLES: With right side facing, work 2 (4–5–6–7–10) sts, k 2 tog, yo, work 3 sts, k 2 tog, yo, work 3 sts. Continue as established until 1 inch above start of shoulder ribbing. Bind off all sts.

SHAPE RIGHT SHOULDER: Leave center 17 (17–19–19–21–21) sts on holder for front neck. Working on remaining sts, dec 1 st at neck edge every other row 2 times. Work even until 5 (5½–5¾–6–6½–7) inches above armhole. Bind off all sts.

NECK BAND: Sew right shoulder seam. With right side facing, using size 3 needles and color B, pick up and k 15 sts on left side of neck, work across 17 (17–19–19–21–21) sts from front holder, pick up and k 15 sts on right side of neck, work across 21 (21–23–23–25–25) sts from back holder, pick up and k 5 sts on shoulder extension. Work on these 73 (73–77–77–81–81) sts in k 1, p 1 rib for ½ inch. On next right-side row, work 2 sts, make 1 one-stitch buttonhole as on shoulder, work across as established. Work in rib until neck band is 1 inch wide. Bind off all sts in rib.

ARMHOLE BANDS: Lap left front shoulder over back shoulder extension and slip-stitch at side edge. With right side facing, using size 3 needles and color B, pick up and k 56 (60–62–66–70–76) sts on armhole and underarm edge. Work in k 1, p 1 rib for 1 inch. Bind off all sts in rib. Repeat procedure for right armhole.

FINISHING: Sew side seams. Sew buttons opposite buttonholes.

□ A
☒ B
⊡ C

FAIR ISLE VEST CHART

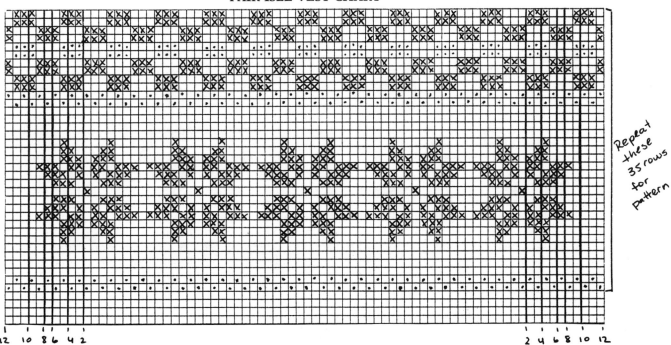

12 10 8 6 4 2   2 4 6 8 10 12

Repeat these 35 rows for pattern

Fair Isle Cardigan

SIZES: Instructions are for size 2. Changes for sizes 4, 6, 8, 10, and 12 are in parentheses. Finished chest measurements are 24 (25½–27–28–29½–32) inches.

MATERIALS: 6 (8–9–9–11–12) oz or 310 (380–425–475–540–615) yds worsted weight Maine wool for color A; 2 (2–3–3–4–4) oz or 100 (100–150–150–200–200) yds color B; 2 oz or 100 yds (all sizes) color C. 1 pair each size 3 and size 4 needles or size needed to obtain gauge; 6 (6–6–7–7–7) ½-inch buttons.

GAUGE: 5 sts = 1 inch.

BACK: With size 3 needles and color A, cast on 56 (60–64–66–70–76) sts. Work in k 1, p 1 rib for 1 (1½–1½–1½–2–2) inches, inc 1 st in last row to make 57 (61–65–67–71–77) sts. With size 4 needles, work even in stockinette stitch (k 1 row, p 1 row) with color A for 4 rows, then follow Chart 1 and repeat last 10 rows of chart until 8 (9½–10–10½–11–11½) inches from beg.

SHAPE ARMHOLE: Following Chart 2, bind off 3 sts at beg of next 2 rows, then dec 1 st at each end of every other row 3 times to leave 45 (49–53–55–59–65) sts. Work even, continuing snowflakes in color C as established until 4¾ (5–5¼–5½–6–6½) inches above armhole.

SHAPE SHOULDER: Bind off 12 (14–15–16–17–20) sts at beg of next row, leave next 21 (21–23–23–25–25) sts on holder for back of neck, bind off remaining sts.

FRONT: With size 3 needles and color A, cast on 28 (30–32–33–35–38) sts. Work in k 1, p 1 rib for 1 (1½–1½–1½–2–2) inches, inc 1 st in last row to make 29 (31–33–34–36–39) sts. Then, with size 4 needles, work even in stockinette stitch, following Chart 1 and Chart 2 as for back.

SHAPE NECK at 2¾ (3–3¼–3½–4–4½) inches above armhole. At center edge, leave 7 (7–8–8–9–9) sts on holder, then at same edge, dec 1 st every other row 4 times to leave 12 (14–15–16–17–20) sts. Work even until same length as back to shoulder. Bind off all sts.

SLEEVES: With size 3 needles and color A, cast on 28 (30–32–34–36–38) sts. Work in k 1, p 1 rib for 1½ (1½–1½–1½–2–2) inches, inc 5 sts evenly in last row to make 33 (35–37–39–41–43) sts. Then, with size 4 needles, work in stockinette stitch following Chart 3 and inc 1 st at each end where indicated on chart, then every 1¾ (1¾–1¾–1¾–1½–1½) inches 3 (4–4–5–6–6) times total to make 39 (43–45–49–53–55) sts, continuing as established when chart is complete. Work even until sleeve measures 9½ (11–12–13–14–15) inches from beg.

SHAPE ARMHOLE AND CAP: Following Chart 4, bind off 3 sts at beg of next 2 rows, then 1 st at each end of every other row until 15 (19–19–21–25–25) sts remain. Then, bind off 3 (4–4–4–3–3) sts at beg of next 4 (4–4–4–6–6) rows. Bind off remaining 3 (3–3–5–7–7) sts.

NECK BAND: Sew shoulder seams. With right side facing and size 3 needles, work across 7 (7–8–8–9–9) sts from front holder, pick up and k 14 sts on right side of neck, work across 21 (21–23–23–

KNITTED BY SUZANNE DESROCHERS

25–25) sts from back holder, pick up and k 14 sts on left side of neck, work across 7 (7–8–8–9–9) sts from front holder. Work on these 63 (63–67–67–71–71) sts in k 1, p 1 rib for 1 inch. Bind off all sts in rib.

BUTTONHOLE BAND: With right side facing, using size 4 needles and color A, pick up and k 59 (67–73–79–81–87) sts on inner edge of left front and work in k 1, p 1 rib for 1 inch. Bind off all sts.

Work in same manner on right front for ½ inch. Then, evenly space 6 (6–6–7–7–7) one-stitch buttonholes in band, having first and last positioned at ½ inch from ends of band. (See Special Techniques chapter for instructions on how to make one-stitch buttonholes.) Work in rib until band is 1 inch wide. Bind off all sts in rib.

FINISHING: Set in sleeves at shoulder. Sew underarm and side seams. Sew buttons.

☐ A
☒ B
· C

FAIR ISLE CARDIGAN CHART 1

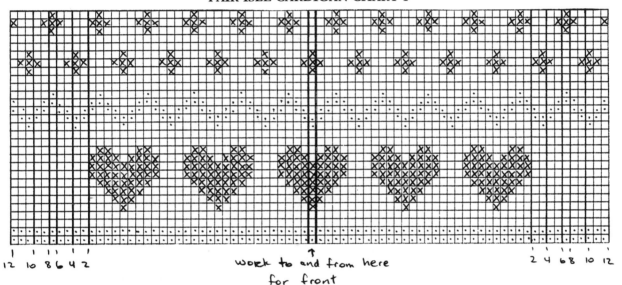

12 10 8 6 4 2   work to and from here for front   2 4 6 8 10 12

FAIR ISLE CARDIGAN CHART 2

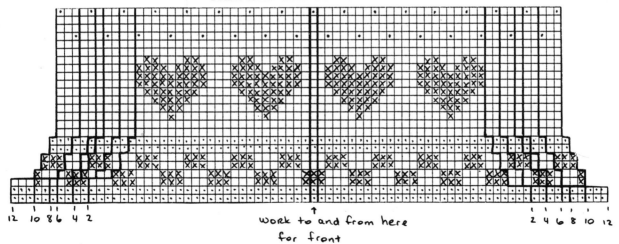

12 10 8 6 4 2   work to and from here for front   2 4 6 8 10 12

FAIR ISLE CARDIGAN CHART 3

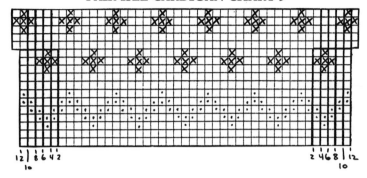

12 | 8 6 4 2
10

2 4 6 8 | 12
10

FAIR ISLE CARDIGAN CHART 4

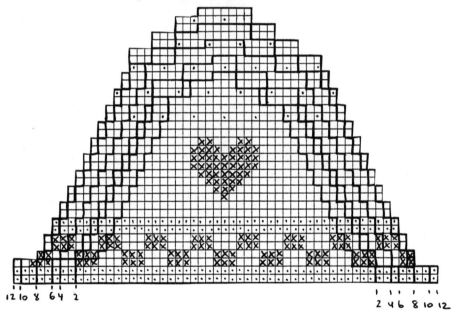

12 10 8 6 4 2

2 4 6 8 10 12

Fair Isle Pullover

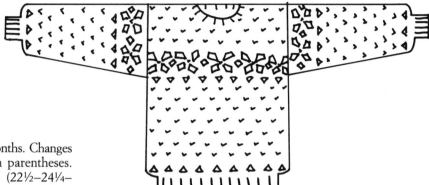

SIZES: Instructions are for size 12 months. Changes for sizes 2, 4, 6, 8, 10, and 12 are in parentheses. Finished chest measurements are 20 (22½–24¼–25¼–26¼–28–30½) inches.

MATERIALS: 5 (6–7–8–9–10–12) oz or 265 (315–370–420–475–525–630) yds worsted weight Maine wool for color A; 2 oz or 100 yds (all sizes) color B; 1 oz or 50 yds (all sizes) color C. 1 pair each size 3 and size 5 needles or size needed to obtain gauge; 1 set size 3 double-pointed needles (dpn).

GAUGE: 4.5 sts = 1 inch.

BACK: With size 3 needles and color A, cast on 44 (50–54–56–58–62–68) sts. Work in k 1, p 1 rib for 1 (1½–1½–1¾–1¾–2–2) inches, inc 1 st in last row to make 45 (51–55–57–59–63–69) sts. Then, with size 5 needles, work in stockinette stitch (k 1 row, p 1 row) for 2 rows. Begin Chart 1, continuing snowflakes in color B as established until 7½ (8–9½–10–10½–11–11½) inches from beg. Place markers at both ends of needle for armhole. Work Chart 2, continuing snowflakes as established when chart is complete until 4¼ (4¾–5–5½–5¾–6–6½) inches above armhole markers.

SHAPE SHOULDERS: Bind off 14 (17–18–19–20–21–24) sts at beg of next row, leave next 17 (17–19–19–19–21–21) sts on holder, bind off remaining sts.

FRONT: Work as for back until 2½ (2¾–3–3½–3¾–4–4½) inches above armhole markers. Shape neck by leaving center 9 (9–11–11–11–13–13) sts on holder, then work both sides at the same time, dec 1 st at neck edges every other row 4 times to leave 14 (17–18–19–20–21–24) sts. Work even until same length to shoulder as back. Bind off all sts.

SLEEVES: Sew shoulder seams. With right side facing, using size 5 needles and color A, pick up and k 39 (43–45–51–53–55–59) sts on armhole edge between markers. Purl back. Work Chart 3, dec 1 st each end on rows indicated on chart, then every ¾ (¾–1–1–1¼–1¼–1¼) inch 7 (9–9–10–10–10–11) times total to leave 25 (25–27–31–33–35–37) sts. Then, at 6 (8–9–10–11–12–13) inches from beg, work Chart 4. Work 2 more rows with color A, decreasing 3 (3–3–5–5–5–5) sts evenly in last row to leave 22 (22–24–26–28–30–32) sts. With size 3 needles, work in k 1, p 1 rib until sleeve measures 7½ (9½–11–12–13–14–15) inches from beg. Bind off all sts in rib.

NECK BAND: With right side facing, using dpn and color A, begin at left shoulder seam and pick up and k 12 sts on side of neck, work across 9 (9–11–11–11–13–13) sts from front holder, pick up and k 12 sts from other side of neck, work across 17 (17–19–19–19–21–21) sts from back holder. Work on these 50 (50–54–54–54–58–58) sts in k 1, p 1 rib for 1 inch. Bind off all sts loosely in rib.

FINISHING: Sew underarm and side seams.

A
B
C

FAIR ISLE PULLOVER CHART 1

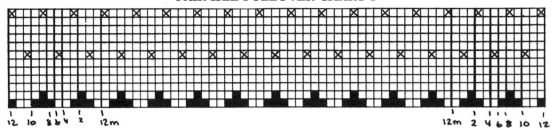

FAIR ISLE PULLOVER CHART 2

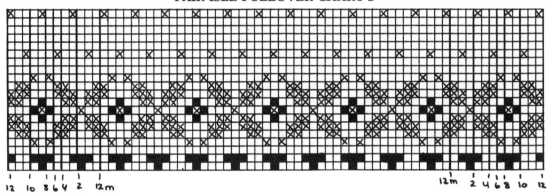

FAIR ISLE PULLOVER CHART 3

FAIR ISLE PULLOVER CHART 4

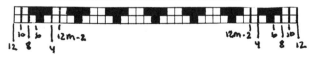

Just for Baby

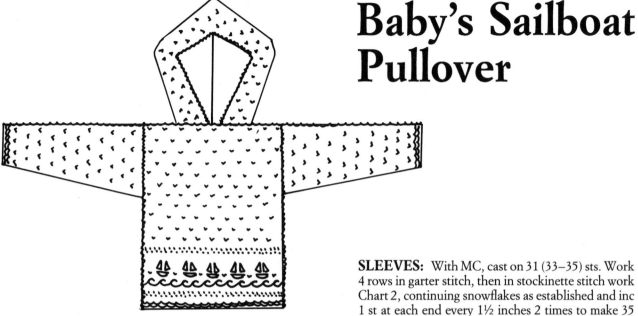

Baby's Sailboat Pullover

SIZES: Instructions are for size 12 months. Changes for sizes 18 and 24 months are in parentheses. Finished chest measurements are 20¼ (22–22¾) inches.

MATERIALS: 6 (7–8) oz or 315 (370–420) yds worsted weight Maine wool for main color (MC); 2 oz or 100 yds (all sizes) contrasting color (CC). 1 pair size 5 needles or size needed to obtain gauge; 1 size F crochet hook; 1 18 (18–20) inch zipper.

GAUGE: 4.5 sts = 1 inch.

BACK: (Make 2 halves. Zipper goes on back of sweater.) With MC, cast on 23 (25–26) sts. Work in garter stitch (k every row) for 4 rows. Then, work in stockinette stitch (k 1 row, p 1 row) for 1 inch. Work Chart 1, continuing snowflakes as established when chart is complete until 7 (7½–8) inches from beg. Place markers on each end of needle for armhole. Work even until 4 (4¼–4½) inches above armhole markers. Bind off all sts.

FRONT: (Make in one piece.) With MC, cast on 45 (49–51) sts. Work as for back until 3½ (3¾–4) inches above armhole markers. Shape neck: Bind off center 21 sts and continue straight on each side of neck opening for ½ inch more. Bind off all sts.

SLEEVES: With MC, cast on 31 (33–35) sts. Work 4 rows in garter stitch, then in stockinette stitch work Chart 2, continuing snowflakes as established and inc 1 st at each end every 1½ inches 2 times to make 35 (37–39) sts. Work until 7 (8–9) inches from beg. Bind off all sts.

HOOD: With MC, cast on 35 sts. Work Chart 3, continuing snowflakes as established until 17 (18–19) inches from beg. Bind off all sts loosely.

FINISHING: All seams are worked in single crochet, with CC, on the outside of the garment. Crochet sides together to markers, then, having sleeves seams facing up, crochet sleeves to armhole edge between markers. Next, crochet sleeves and shoulder seams. Crochet hood to body, having front edges 1 inch apart at neck opening and back edges even with back opening. Then, work 1 row single crochet around center edge of back and hood. Sew on zipper. (Zipper is slightly shorter than back opening, so the 2 or 3 inches left open at the top of hood should be slip-stitched together.)

BABY'S SAILBOAT PULLOVER CHART 1

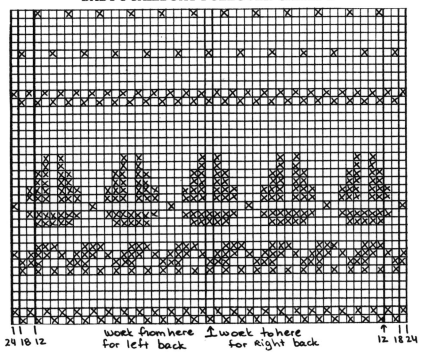

24 18 12   work from here   ↑ work to here   12 18 24
             for left back   for right back

BABY'S SAILBOAT PULLOVER CHART 2

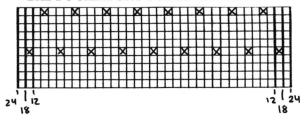

24 12   12 24
  18   18

□ MAIN COLOR
☒ CONTRAST COLOR

BABY'S SAILBOAT PULLOVER CHART 3

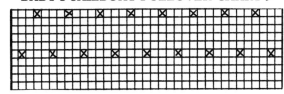

Baby's Cardigan, Hat,& Mittens

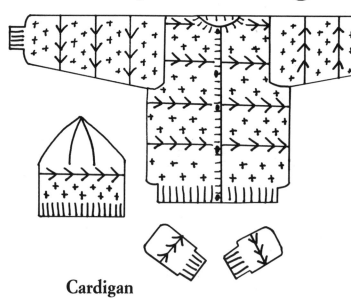

Cardigan

SIZES: Instructions are for size 6 months. Changes for sizes 12, 18, and 24 months are in parentheses. Finished chest measurements are 20½ (21–21¾–22½) inches.

MATERIALS: 4 (5–6–7) oz or 220 (260–310–350) yds worsted weight washable wool for main color (MC); 2 (2–2–3) oz or 75 (85–95–105) yds contrasting color (CC). 1 pair each size 3 and size 5 needles or size needed to obtain gauge; 5 ½-inch buttons.

GAUGE: 5.5 sts = 1 inch.

BACK: With size 3 needles and MC, cast on 52 (54–56–58) sts. Work in k 1, p 1 rib for 1 inch, inc 1 st in last row to make 53 (55–57–59) sts. Then, with size 5 needles, in stockinette stitch (k 1 row, p 1 row), begin Chart 1, repeating these 22 rows for rest of back. At the same time, at 6½ (7–7½–8) inches from beg, shape armhole.

ARMHOLE: Bind off 3 sts at beg of next 2 rows, then dec 1 st at each end of every other row 2 times to leave 43 (45–47–49) sts. Work even until 3¾ (4–4¼–4½) inches above armhole.

SHAPE SHOULDER: Bind off 13 (13–14–14) sts, leave next 17 (19–19–21) sts on holder for back of neck, bind off remaining sts.

LEFT FRONT: With size 3 needles and MC, cast on 26 (28–28–30) sts. Work in k 1, p 1 rib for 1 inch, inc 1 (0–1–0) st in last row to make 27 (28–29–30) sts. Then, with size 5 needles, in stockinette stitch, begin Chart 1, making sure to shape armhole where required, as for back.

SHAPE NECK: At 1¾ (2–2¼–2½) inches above armhole, leave 4 (5–5–6) sts on holder at neck edge, then at same edge, dec 1 st every other row 5 times to leave 13 (13–14–14) sts. Work even until same depth as back to shoulder. Bind off all sts.

RIGHT FRONT: Work as for left, reversing shaping.

SLEEVES: With size 3 needles and MC, cast on 22 (24–26–28) sts. Work in k 1, p 1 rib for 1½ inches, inc 5 sts evenly in last row to make 27 (29–31–33) sts. Then, with size 5 needles, in stockinette stitch, begin Chart 2, inc 1 st at each end on row 11, then inc every 1 (1¼–1½–1¾) inch 3 times more to make 35 (37–39–41) sts. Work even until 6½ (7½–8½–9½) inches from beg, or desired length to underarm.

SHAPE ARMHOLE AND CAP: Bind off 3 sts at beg of next 2 rows, then dec 1 st at each end of every other row until 17 sts remain. Bind off 3 sts at beg of next 4 rows. Bind off remaining 5 sts.

NECK BAND: Sew shoulder seams. With right side facing, using size 3 needles and MC, work across 4 (5–5–6) sts from front holder, pick up and k 14 sts on side of neck, work across 17 (19–19–21) sts from back holder, pick up and k 14 sts on side of neck, work across 4 (5–5–6) sts from front holder. Work on these 53 (57–57–61) sts in k 1, p 1 rib for ¾ inch. Bind off all sts in rib.

FRONT BUTTON BANDS: With right side facing, using size 5 needles and MC, pick up and k 49 (53–57–61) sts on front edge. Work in k 1, p 1 rib for ½ inch. Work 5 one-stitch buttonholes evenly spaced (on left front for boys, right front for girls), working first and last ones ½ inch from ends of band. (See Special Techniques chapter for instructions on how to make one-stitch buttonholes.) Work for ½ inch more, then bind off all sts.

FINISHING: Set in sleeves. Sew underarm and side seams. Sew on buttons.

Hat and Mittens

MATERIALS: 2 (3–4) oz or 110 (150–190 yds) worsted weight wool for MC; 1 oz or 50 yds (all sizes) CC. 1 set each size 3 and size 5 double-pointed needles (dpn) or size needed to obtain gauge.

GAUGE: 5.5 sts = 1 inch.

Hat

SIZES: Instructions are for size small (15¼ inches). Changes for sizes medium (17½ inches) and large (19½ inches) are in parentheses.

BABY'S CARDIGAN CHART 1

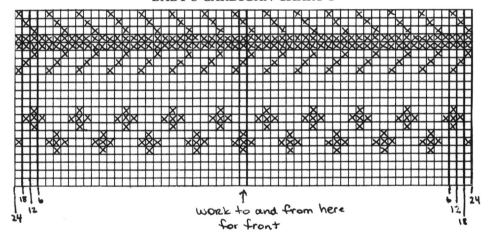

□ MAIN COLOR
☒ CONTRAST COLOR

work to and from here for front

BABY'S CARDIGAN CHART 2

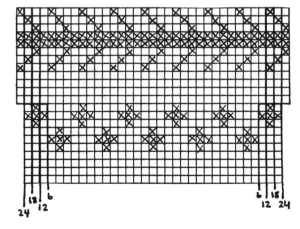

BABY'S HAT OR MITTENS CHART

BABY'S HAT CHART

RIBBING AND PATTERN: With size 3 dpn and MC, cast on 84 (96–108) sts. Work in k 1, p 1 rib for 1½ (1¾–2) inches. Then, with size 5 dpn, k 4 rows MC, k 6 rows of Hat Chart, k 4 rows MC, k 8 rows of Hat or Mitten Chart. Continue with MC only, knitting every row until 5 (5½–6) inches from beg.

SHAPE CAP: *K 10, k 2 tog*, repeat between * across row. K next row. Then, *k 9, k 2 tog*, repeat between * across row. K next row. Continue in this manner, working decreases every other row as established until 7 (8–9) sts remain. Slip yarn through these last sts and draw up tightly. Darn end of yarn into wrong side. Make pompom and sew in place.

Thumbless Mittens

SIZES: Instructions are for size small. Changes for sizes medium and large are in parentheses.

CUFF: With size 3 dpn, cast on 24 (28–30) sts. Work in k 1, p 1 rib for 1½ (2–2½) inches, inc 4 (4–6) sts evenly in last row to make 28 (32–36) sts.

HAND: With size 5 dpn, k 4 rows MC, k 8 rows of Hat or Mittens Chart. Continue with MC only, knitting every row until 3½ (4½–5½) inches from beg.

SHAPE TOP: Row 1: [K 1, k 2 tog, k 9 (11–13), k 2 tog] 2 times. Row 2: [K 1, k 2 tog, k 7 (9–11), k 2 tog] 2 times. Row 3: [K 1, k 2 tog, k 5 (7–9), k 2 tog] 2 times. Row 4: [K 1, k 2 tog, k 3 (5–7), k 2 tog] 2 times. Divide remaining 12 (16–20) sts evenly in 2 and weave sts together across tip of mitten.

Baby Bunting

KNITTED BY RHODA LIBBY

MATERIALS: 7 oz or 380 yds worsted weight washable wool color A; 3 oz or 175 yds color B; 2 oz or 100 yds each colors C and D. 1 pair each size 3 and size 5 needles or size needed to obtain gauge; 1 size H crochet hook; 1 9-inch zipper.

GAUGE: 5.5 sts = 1 inch, 7 rows = 1 inch in snowflake stitch.

BACK: With size 5 needles and color B, cast on 85 sts. Working in stockinette stitch (k 1 row, p 1 row), begin Chart 1, decreasing 1 st at each end every eighth row as indicated on chart. Continue snowflake pattern and decreases in the same manner until 55

SIZES: Instructions are for size newborn (0 to 3 months). Finished chest measurement is 20 inches.

sts remain. At the same time, when ready to work snowflakes on chart, work snowflake stitch as follows: on a right-side row, k snowflake with color B as indicated, and on next wrong-side row, k again in st right above snowflake with the same color, thus forming a purl st in the right side of work. Continue snowflakes as established, repeating color sequence (B, C, D) as shown, for rest of piece.

BABY BUNTING CHART 1

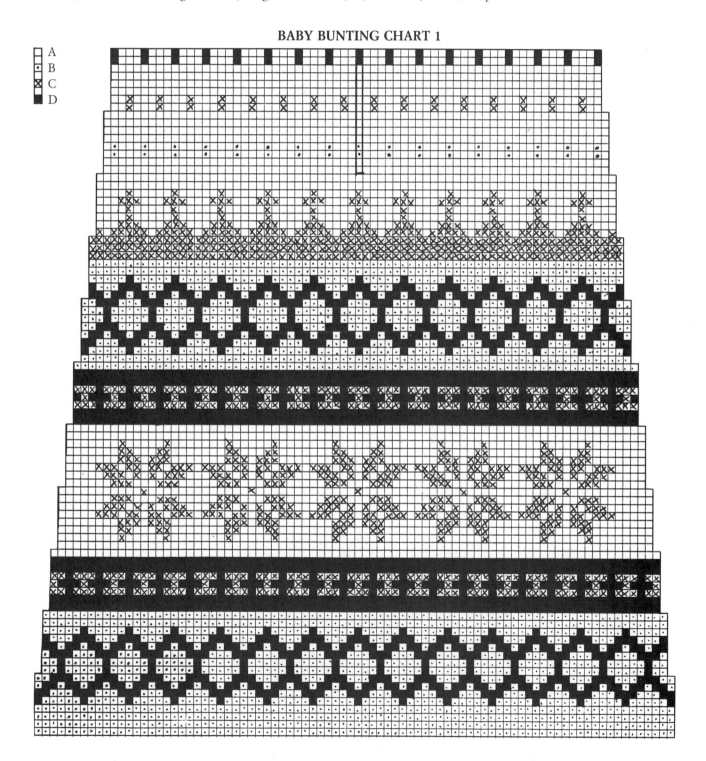

SHAPE ARMHOLE: At 17 inches from beg, bind off 3 sts at beg of next 2 rows. Then, dec 1 st at each end of every other row 3 times to leave 43 sts. Work even until 4 inches above armhole.

SHAPE SHOULDER: Bind off 11 sts, leave next 21 sts on holder for back of neck, bind off next 11 10s.

FRONT: Work as for back, binding off center st before starting snowflakes, as indicated on chart. Attach a second ball of yarn and work both sides at the same time, shaping armhole where required. Work until 3 inches above armhole. Then, at neck edge, leave 8 sts on holder for front of neck, and at same edge, dec 1 st every other row 2 times. Bind off all sts when front measures same length as back to shoulder.

SLEEVES: With size 3 needles and color A, cast on 28 sts. Work in k 1, p 1 rib for 1 inch, inc 5 sts evenly in last row to make 33 sts. Then, work Chart 2, inc 1 st at each end every 10 rows as indicated on chart. Continue these increases as established to make 39 sts, and work snowflakes color sequence as for back.

SHAPE ARMHOLE AND CAP: At 6½ inches from beg, bind off 3 sts at beg of next 2 rows, then dec 1 st at each end of every other row until 15 sts remain. Bind off 3 sts at beg of next 4 rows. Bind off remaining 3 sts.

HOOD: Sew shoulder seams. With size 5 needles and color A, work across 8 sts from right front holder, pick up and k 10 sts on side of neck, work across 21 sts from back holder, pick up and k 10 sts on side of neck, work across 8 sts from left front holder. Purl back. Work on these 57 sts as follows: Work in garter stitch (k every row) on first and last 5 sts, and in stockinette stitch on center 47 sts, following Chart 3 for snowflakes placement and following same color sequence as for back. Work even until 7 inches from beg. Bind off all sts.

FINISHING: Fold hood in half and sew top edges together. With crochet hook and color B, work 1 row of single crochet around front edge of hood and front opening. Set in sleeves at shoulder. Sew underarm, side, and bottom seams. Sew in zipper. Weave in all ends.

BABY BUNTING CHART 2

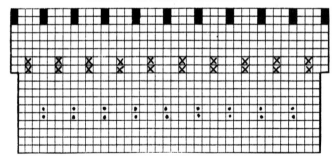

BABY BUNTING CHART 3

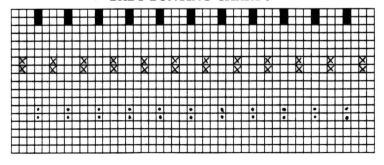

Moose Cardigan, Moose Pullover, Deer Pullover, and Rabbit Pullover.

Sailboat Pullover and Whale Hooded Pullover.

Lighthouse Pullover and Puffin Pullover.

Aran Cardigan, Aran Vest, and Aran Pullover.

Pine Tree Pullover, Blueberry Vest, and Blueberry Cardigan.

Fair Isle Vest, Fair Isle Cardigan, and Fair Isle Pullover.

Sheep Pullover and Bear Pullover.

Baby's Cardigan, Hat, and Mittens, Baby Bunting, and Baby's Sailboat Pullover.

Penguin Pullover, Sampler Pullover, and Panda Pullover. ▶

Girl's Daisy Cardigan, Tree of Life Pullover, and Cabled Turtleneck. ▼

Girl's Wool and Mohair Coat and Boy's Pullover. ▶

Animals
and
More Animals

Bear Pullover

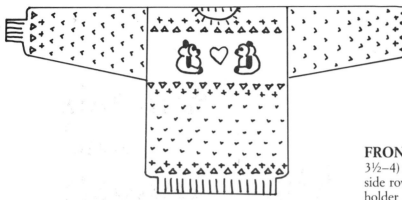

SIZES: Instructions are for size 12 months. Changes for sizes 2, 4, 6, 8, and 10 are in parentheses. Finished chest measurements are 20½ (22–24½–25¼–26–27½) inches.

MATERIALS: 5 (6–7–8–9–10) oz or 265 (315–370–420–475–525) yds worsted weight Maine wool for main color (MC); 2 oz or 100 yds each (all sizes) Bartlettyarns Natural, Medium Sheep's Grey, and Dark Sheep's Grey. 1 pair each size 3 and size 5 needles or size needed to obtain gauge.

GAUGE: 5 sts = 1 inch.

BACK: With size 3 needles and MC, cast on 48 (52–58–60–62–66) sts. Work in k 1, p 1 rib for 1¼ (1¼–1½–1½–1¾–1¾) inches, inc 3 sts evenly in last row to make 51 (55–61–63–65–69) sts. With size 5 needles, work 2 rows stockinette stitch (k 1 row, p 1 row) with MC only, then begin working Chart 1, continuing snowflakes as established when chart is complete until 6 (7–8½–9–9½–10) inches from beg. Then, work Chart 2 for 1 inch, place markers at both ends of needle for armhole. Continue Chart 2, working with MC only when chart is complete, until 4¼ (4½–5–5¼–5½–6) inches above armhole markers.

SHAPE SHOULDER: Bind off 5 (6–7–7–7–8) sts at beg of next 4 rows, 6 (6–7–7–8–7) sts at beg of next 2 rows. Leave remaining 19 (19–19–21–21–23) sts on holder for back of neck.

FRONT: Work as for back until 2½ (3–3½–3½–3½–4) inches above armhole markers. On next right-side row, leave center 11 (11–11–13–13–13) sts on holder for neck. Then, using two balls of yarn and working both sides at the same time, dec 1 st at neck edge every other row 4 (4–4–4–4–5) times to leave 16 (18–21–21–22–23) sts. When armhole is same depth to shoulder as back, shape as for back.

SLEEVES: With size 3 needles and MC, cast on 24 (28-32-34-36-38) sts. Work in k 1, p 1 rib for 1½ (1½-1½-1½-2-2) inches, inc 5 sts evenly in last row to make 29 (33-37-39-41-43) sts. With size 5 needles, work 2 rows in stockinette stitch with MC only, then begin working Chart 3, inc 1 st at each end where indicated on the chart, then every 1¼ (1¼-1½-1¼-1½-1¼) inches 5 (6-6-7-7-8) times total, to make 39 (45-49-53-55-59) sts. Work even, keeping snowflakes as established, until 8 (10-11-12-13-14) inches from beg, or desired length to underarm. Bind off all sts.

NECK BAND: Sew right shoulder seam. With size 3 needles and MC, pick up and k 13 (13-13-15-15-15) sts on side of neck, work across 11 (11-11-13-13-13) sts from front holder, pick up and k 13 (13-13-15-15-15) sts on side of neck, work across 19 (19-19-21-21-23) sts from back holder. Work on these 56 (56-56-64-64-66) sts in k 1, p 1, rib for ¾ inch. Bind off all sts in rib (make sure to bind off loosely so neck band will be stretchy enough for child's head to pass easily).

FINISHING: Sew side of neck band and left shoulder seam. Set in sleeves between markers. Sew underarm and side seams.

KNITTED BY THEO HEALD

BEAR PULLOVER CHART 1

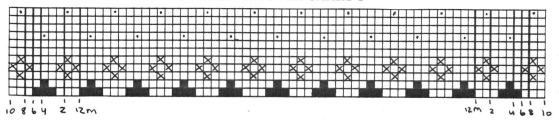

10 8 6 4 2 12m   12m 2 4 6 8 10

BEAR PULLOVER CHART 2

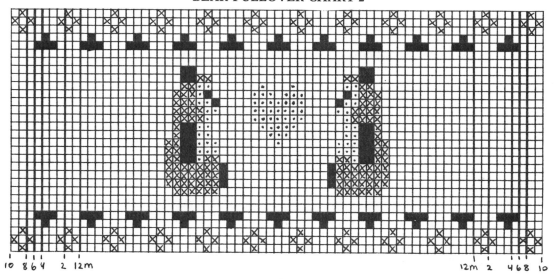

10 8 6 4 2 12m   12m 2 4 6 8 10

BEAR PULLOVER CHART 3

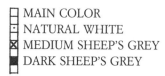

MAIN COLOR
NATURAL WHITE
MEDIUM SHEEP'S GREY
DARK SHEEP'S GREY

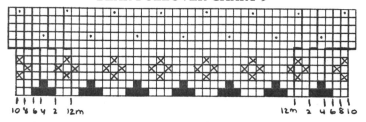

10 8 6 4 2 12m   12m 2 4 6 8 10

Sheep Pullover

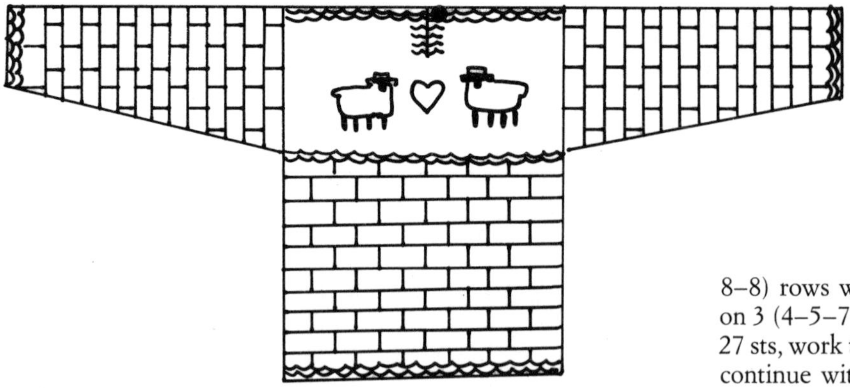

SIZES: Instructions are for size 12 months. Changes for sizes 18 months, 2, 4, 6, 8, 10, and 12 are in parentheses. Finished chest measurements are 19½ (20½–21¾–24–25–26¼–28½–29¾)inches.

MATERIALS: 6 (7–7–9–10–11–13–15) oz or 190 (235–245–315–350–385–445–510) yds bulky weight Maine wool for main color (MC); 25 yards Bartlett-yarns Natural and 10 yards Dark Sheep's Grey. 1 pair each size 8 and size 10 needles or size needed to obtain gauge. 1 size G crochet hook. 1 ¾-inch button.

GAUGE: 3.5 sts = 1 inch in Basketweave Stitch.

Basketweave Stitch
Rows 1 and 7 (right side facing): K
Rows 2 and 8: P
Row 3: *K 1, p 4, k 1*, repeat between * across.
Rows 4, 5, and 6: K on k, p on p.
Row 9: *K 2, p 2, k 2*, repeat between * across.
Rows 10, 11, and 12: K on k, p on p.
Repeat these 12 rows for pattern.

BACK: With size 8 needles and MC, cast on 34 (36–38–42–44–46–50–52) sts. Work in garter stitch (k every row) for 6 rows. Then, with size 10 needles, work in basketweave stitch (note: pattern will not be distributed evenly across row for all sizes, so be sure to k on k, p on p on indicated rows) until 6½ (7–7½–9–9½–10–10½–11) inches from beg. Work 4 rows of garter stitch, dec 1 st in last row to leave 33 (35–37–41–43–45–49–51) sts. Then, work in stockinette stitch (k 1 row, p 1 row) for 2 (2–4–4–6–6–8–8) rows with MC. On next right-side row, work on 3 (4–5–7–8–9–11–12) sts, work Chart on center 27 sts, work to end of row. When Chart is completed, continue with MC only until 3½ (3¾–4–4½–4¾–5–5½ –6) inches above start of yoke. Work in garter stitch for ½ inch more. Bind off all sts.

FRONT: Work as for back until 2½ (2¾–3–3¼–3½–3¾–4–4½) inches above start of yoke. On next right-side row, work across 16 (17–18–20–21–22–24–25) sts, bind off center st, work to end of row. Then, with wrong side facing, and working both sides at the same time, purl across to 3 sts before center edge, work these 3 sts in garter stitch (k every row). Work as established, keeping center edge sts in garter stitch until yoke measures 3½ (3¾–4–4½–4¾–5–5½ –6) inches. Then, work in garter stitch on all sts for ½ inch. Bind off all sts.

SLEEVES: Sew shoulder seams, leaving a 6 (6–6½–6½–7–7–7¼–7¼) inch neck opening. With right side facing and using size 10 needles, pick up and k 28 (30–32–36–36–38–42–46) sts on yoke edge. Begin work with row 2 of basketweave stitch, decreasing 1 st at each end every 3 (3–2½–2¼–2½–2¾–2–1¾) inches 2 (2–3–4–4–4–6–7) times to leave 24 (26–26–28–28–30–30–32) sts. Work even until sleeve measures 6½ (7½–8½–10–11–12–13–14)inches from beg. Then, with size 8 needles, work in garter stitch for 1 inch. Bind off all sts.

FINISHING: Sew underarm and side seams. With crochet hook, work 1 buttonloop at neck edge (left side for boys, right for girls). Sew button.

SHEEP PULLOVER CHART

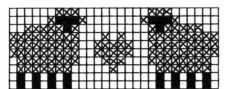

⊠ NATURAL WHITE
■ DARK SHEEP'S GREY

Penguin Pullover

SIZES: Instructions are for size 2. Changes for sizes 4, 6, 8, and 10 are in parentheses. Finished chest measurements are 22 (24–26–28–30) inches.

MATERIALS: 6 (8–9–10–11) oz or 330 (405–450–515–590) yds worsted weight washable wool for main color (MC); 1 (1–2–2–2) oz or 45 (55–60–70–80) yds each white and black; 10 yards yellow. 1 pair each size 3 and size 5 needles or size needed to obtain gauge.

GAUGE: 5.5 sts = 1 inch.

BACK: With size 3 needles and MC, cast on 58 (64–66–68–74) sts. Work in k 1, p 1 rib for 1½ inches, inc 3 sts evenly in last row to make 61 (67–69–71–77) sts. Then, with size 5 needles, work 3 rows stockinette stitch (k 1 row, p 1 row). Next, with wrong side facing, work Chart 1. Work 4 rows of stockinette stitch with MC. Then, begin working penguins as follows: MC on 4 (7–8–2–5) sts, (Chart 2 followed by MC on 3 sts) 3 (3–3–4–4) times, Chart 2, MC on 4 (7–8–2–5) sts—you will have 4 (4–4–5–5) penguins across. When Chart 2 is complete, work 4 rows MC, then begin working Chart 3, continuing snowflakes as established until 8 (9½–10–

10½–11)inches from beg, or desired length to underarm.

SHAPE ARMHOLE: Bind off 4 sts at beg of next 2 rows, then dec 1 st at each end of every other row 3 times to make 47 (53–55–57–63) sts. Work even until 4¾ (5–5¼–5½–6) inches above armhole, then bind off 13 (16–16–17–19) sts, leave next 21 (21–23–23–25) sts on holder for back of neck, bind off remaining sts.

FRONT: Work as for back until 2¾ (3–3¼–3½–4) inches above armhole. Shape neck on next right-side row: leave center 13 (13–15–15–17) sts on holder, then, working both sides at the same time, dec 1 st at neck edge of every other row 4 times to leave 13 (16–16–17–19) sts. When armhole is same depth as back to shoulder, bind off all sts.

SLEEVES: With size 3 needles and MC, cast on 28 (30–32–34–36) sts. Work in k 1, p 1, rib for 1½ inches, inc 5 sts evenly in last row to make 33 (35–

37–39–41) sts. Work in stockinette stitch with size 5 needles for 3 rows. Then, with wrong side facing, work Chart 4. Continue working snowflakes as established, inc 1 st each side on first row of snowflakes, then every 1½ inches 4 (5–5–6–7) times more to make 43 (47–49–53–57) sts. Work even until 10 (11–12–13–14) inches from beg, or desired length to underarm.

SHAPE ARMHOLE AND CAP: Bind off 4 sts at beg of next 2 rows, then dec 1 st at each end of every other row until 17 sts remain. Bind off 3 sts at beg of next 4 rows. Bind off remaining 5 sts.

NECK BAND: Sew right shoulder seam. Then, with right side facing, using size 3 needles and MC, pick up and k 14 sts from left side of neck, work across 13 (13–15–15–17) sts from front holder, pick up and k 14 sts from right side of neck, work across 21 (21–23–23–25) sts from back holder. Work on these 62 (62–66–66–70) sts in k 1, p 1 rib for 1½ inches. Bind off loosely in rib.

FINISHING: Sew side of neck and left shoulder seam. Fold neck band in half to inside and slip-stitch loosely in place. Set in sleeves and sew underarm and side seams.

PENGUIN PULLOVER CHART 1

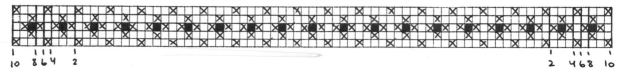

PENGUIN PULLOVER CHART 2

☐ MAIN COLOR
☒ WHITE
■ BLACK
⊡ YELLOW

PENGUIN PULLOVER CHART 3

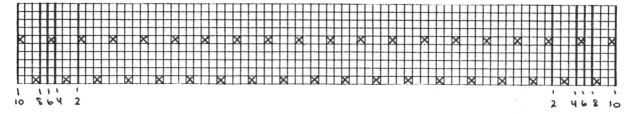

PENGUIN PULLOVER CHART 4

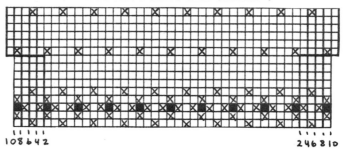

Panda Pullover

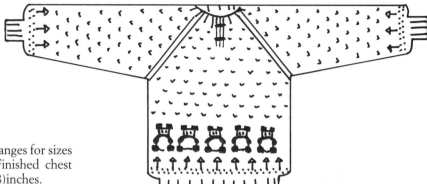

SIZES: Instructions are for size 2. Changes for sizes 4, 6, 8, and 10 are in parentheses. Finished chest measurements are 22 (24¼–25–26–28)inches.

MATERIALS: 6 (8–9–10–11) oz or 330 (405–450–515–590) yds worsted weight washable wool for main color (MC); 1 (1–2–2–2) oz or 45 (55–60–70–80) yds each white and black. 1 pair each size 3 and size 5 needles or size needed to obtain gauge, 1 size 3 16-inch circular needle; 2 ½-inch buttons.

GAUGE: 5.5 sts = 1 inch, 7 rows = 1 inch.

BACK: With size 3 needles and MC, cast on 58 (64–66–68–74) sts. Work in k 1, p 1 rib for 1½ inches, inc 3 sts evenly in last row to make 61 (67–69–71–77) sts. Then, with size 5 needles, in stockinette stitch (k 1 row, p 1 row), work 4 rows with MC. Work Chart 1. Work 4 rows of stockinette stitch with MC. Then begin working pandas as follows: MC on 2 (5–6–1–4) sts, (Chart 2 followed by MC on 3 sts) 4 (4–4–5–5) times, end Chart 2, MC on 2 (5–6–1–4) sts—you will have 5 (5–5–6–6) pandas across. When Chart 2 is complete, work 4 rows MC, then begin working Chart 3, continuing snowflakes as established until 8 (9½–10–10½–11)inches from beg, or desired length to underarm.

SHAPE ARMHOLE: Bind off 2 (4–3–3–3) sts at beg of next 2 rows, then work next right-side row as follows: K 1, k 2 tog, work to last 3 sts, sl 1, k 1, psso, k 1. Purl back. Repeat these last 2 rows until 21 (21–23–23–25) sts remain. Leave these on holder for back of neck.

FRONT AND LEFT SHOULDER: Work as for back until 47 (47–49–49–51) sts remain above armhole. Begin placket band: With right side facing, k 1, k 2 tog, k 18 (18–19–19–20) sts. Leave remaining sts on holder. Turn, and cast on 5 sts at beg of next row. Work in k 1, p 1 rib on these 5 sts, then work to end of row as established. At ¾ inch above start of band, work a one-stitch buttonhole in center of band (if making a girl's pullover, work this buttonhole in right band instead). (See Special Techniques chapter for instructions on one-stitch buttonholes.) Continue left shoulder as established, making sure to shape armhole as required until 2¾ (3–3¼–3½–4) inches above armhole.

SHAPE NECK: Leave 7 (7–8–8–9) sts on holder at neck edge for front of neck. Then, dec 1 st at neck edge every other row 5 times. Work until 1 st remains. Bind off.

RIGHT SHOULDER: Work in k 1, p 1 rib on first 5 sts from holder, then work to end of row, making sure to shape armhole edge as established. Complete this side as for left side, reversing shaping.

SLEEVES: With size 3 needles and MC, cast on 28 (30–32–34–36) sts. Work in k 1, p 1 rib for 1½ inches, inc 5 sts evenly in last row to make 33 (35–37–39–41) sts. Work in stockinette stitch with size 5 needles for 4 rows, then work Chart 4. Continue working snowflakes as established, inc 1 st at each side of first row of snowflakes, then every 1½ inches 4 (5–5–6–7) times more to make 43 (47–49–53–57) sts.

Work even until 10 (11–12–13–14) inches from beg, or desired length to underarm.

SHAPE ARMHOLE AND CAP: Bind off 2 (3–3–3–3) sts at beg of next 2 rows, then work armhole shaping as for back until 3 (3–3–5–5) sts remain. Leave on holder.

NECK BAND: Sew all shoulder seams. Then, with right side facing, using circular needle and MC, work across 7 (7–8–8–9) sts from front holder in k 1, p 1 rib, pick up and k 13 sts on side of neck, work

across 3 (3–3–5–5) sts from sleeve holder, work across 21 (21–23–23–25) sts from back holder, work across 3 (3–3–5–5) sts from sleeve holder, pick up and k 13 sts on side of neck, work across 7 (7–8–8–9) sts from front holder in k 1, p 1 rib. Work on these 67 (67–71–75–79) sts in k 1, p 1 rib for ¼ inch. Work 2nd buttonhole in center of band, work for ½ inch more. Bind off in rib.

FINISHING: Sew underarm and side seams. Slip-stitch buttonhole band edge to inside. Weave in all ends. Sew buttons.

PANDA PULLOVER CHART 1

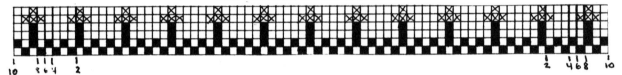

☐ MAIN COLOR
■ BLACK
☒ WHITE

PANDA PULLOVER CHART 2

PANDA PULLOVER CHART 3

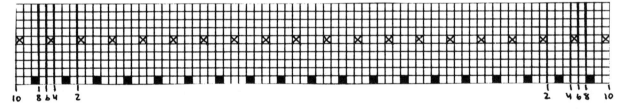

PANDA PULLOVER CHART 4

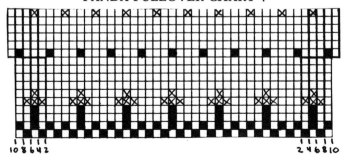

Rabbit Pullover

SIZES: Instructions are for size 2. Changes for sizes 4, 6, 8, 10, and 12 are in parentheses. Finished chest measurements are 22½ (24–25½–26½–28–30½) inches.

MATERIALS: 7 (8–9–11–12–14) oz or 370 (420–475–580–630–735) yards worsted weight Maine wool for main color (MC); 5 yards green Maine wool; 15 yards angora for rabbits. 1 pair each size 2 and size 4 needles or size needed to obtain gauge.

GAUGE: 5 sts = 1 inch.

BACK: With size 2 needles and MC, cast on 54 (58–62–64–68–74) sts. Work in k 1, p 1 rib for 1 (1½–1½–1½–2–2) inches, inc 2 sts evenly in last row to make 56 (60–64–66–70–76) sts. Then, with size 4 needles, work even in stockinette stitch (k 1 row, p 1 row) until 8 (9½–10–10½–11–11½) inches from beg.

SHAPE ARMHOLE: Bind off 3 sts at beg of next 2 rows, then dec 1 st at each end of every other row 3 times to leave 44 (48–52–54–58–64) sts. Work even until 4¾ (5–5¼–5½–6–6½)inches above armhole.

SHAPE SHOULDER: Bind off 12 (14–15–16–17–20) sts at beg of next row, leave next 20 (20–22–22–24–24) sts on holder for back of neck, bind off remaining sts.

FRONT: Work as for back until lower ribbing is complete. Work 4 rows of stockinette stitch in MC. Then work chart, shaping armhole and neck at 8 (9½–10–10½–11–11½) inches from beg (in the smaller sizes this may be before chart is complete).

KNITTED BY LANA BRADBURY

Note: Angora yarn is less stretchy than wool, so be sure to knit the angora sections with loose tension to prevent puckering around the rabbit motifs.

SHAPE NECK: Divide sts evenly in 2, attach a second ball of yarn, and work both sides at the same time. Dec 1 st at neck edge every ⅓ inch until 12 (14–15–16–17–20) sts remain. Work even until same depth as back to shoulder. Bind off all sts.

SLEEVES: With size 2 needles and MC, cast on 28 (30–32–34–36–38) sts. Work in k 1, p 1 rib for 1½ (1½–1½–1½–2–2)inches, inc 6 (5–5–4–5–5) sts evenly in last row to make 34 (35–37–38–41–43) sts. Then, with size 4 needles, work in stockinette stitch, inc 1 st at each end every 1¾ inches 2 (4–4–5–6–6) times to make 38 (43–45–48–53–55) sts. Work even until sleeve measures 9½ (11–12–13–14–15)inches from beg.

SHAPE ARMHOLE AND CAP: Bind off 3 sts at beg of next 2 rows, then 1 st at each end of every other row until 16 (19–19–20–25–25) sts remain. Then, bind off 3 (4–4–4–3–3) sts at beg of next 4 (4–4–4–6–6) rows. Bind off remaining 4 (3–3–4–7–7) sts.

NECK BAND: Sew right shoulder seam. With right side facing, and using size 2 needles, pick up and k 34 (35–36–37–40–42) sts on left side of neck, pick up 1 st in center of V, pick up and k 34 (35–36–37–40–42) sts on right side of neck, work across 20 (20–20–22–22–24) sts from back holder. Work on these 89 (91–93–97–103–109) sts in k 1, p 1 rib, dec 1 st on each side of st in center of V every row until band measures 1 inch wide (be sure to k st in center of **V** on the right side and p it on the wrong side). Bind off all sts in rib.

FINISHING: Sew left side of neck band and left shoulder seam. Set in sleeves at shoulder. Sew under-arm and side seams.

⊠ ANGORA
■ GREEN

RABBIT PULLOVER CHART

More Custom Designs

Sampler Pullover

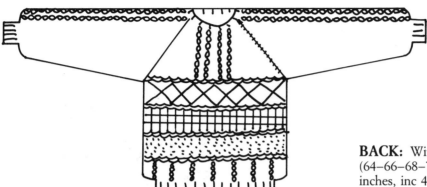

SIZES: Instructions are for size 2. Changes for sizes 4, 6, 8, and 10 are in parentheses. Finished chest measurements are 22 (24–25–26–28) inches.

MATERIALS: 8 (10–11–13–14) oz or 435 (535–595–665–765) yds washable wool; 1 pair each size 3 and size 5 needles or size needed to obtain gauge; 1 7-inch zipper (optional for larger sizes).

GAUGE: 5.5 sts = 1 inch, 7 rows = 1 inch.

STITCHES USED

Pattern #1

Row 1: *K 6, p 1, k 2, p 1*. Repeat between *, end with k 6.

Rows 2 and 4: K on k, p on p.

Row 3: *K 6, p 1, [baby cable: skip next st, k second st but leave on needle, k skipped st, drop both sts together off left needle], p 1*. Repeat between * across, end with k 6.

Pattern #2

Row 1: K 1, p 1.

Rows 2 and 4: K on k, p on p.

Row 3: P 1, k 1.

Pattern #3

Rows 1 and 3: K 4, p 4.

Row 2 and all wrong-side rows: K on k, p on p.

Rows 5 and 7: P 4, k 4.

Pattern #4

Rows 1 and 3: *baby cable (see pattern #1 above) on 2 sts, p 2*. Repeat between *, end with baby cable on 2 sts.

Rows 2 and 4: K on k, p on p.

BACK: With size 3 needles and MC, cast on 58 (64–66–68–74) sts. Work in k 1, p 1 rib for 1½ inches, inc 4 sts evenly in last row to make 62 (68–70–72–78) sts. Then, with size 5 needles, work as follows: Stockinette stitch (k 1 row, p 1 row) on 3 (1–2–3–1) sts, pattern #1 on 56 (66–66–66–76) sts, stockinette stitch on 3 (1–2–3–1) sts. Work as established for 1¼ (1¾–1¼–2–2) inches. Work 4 rows of garter stitch (k every row). Next, work in pattern #2 for 1¼ (1¾–1¼–2–2) inches. Work 4 rows of garter stitch. Then, work as follows: stockinette stitch on 1 (0–1–0–1) st, pattern #3 on 60 (68–68–72–76) sts, stockinette stitch on 1 (0–1–0–1) st. Work as established for 1¼ (1¾–1¼–2–2) inches. Work 4 rows garter stitch, decreasing 1 st in last row. Next, work chart, purling Xs on the right-side rows of stockinette stitch. When chart is complete, work 4 rows of garter stitch, increasing 1 st in first row.

SHAPE ARMHOLE: Bind off 2 (4–3–3–3) sts at beg of next row, work in reverse stockinette stitch (p 1 row, k 1 row) across 22 (23–25–26–29) sts, work pattern #4 on next 14 sts, work to end of row. Bind off 2 (4–3–3–3) sts at beg of next row and work across as established. Then, keeping pattern constant, on every right-side row work as follows: K 1, k 2 tog, work to last 3 sts, sl 1, k 1, psso, k 1. On wrong side, k on k, p on p. Repeat these last 2 rows until 22 (22–24–24–26) sts remain. Leave on holder for back of neck.

FRONT: Work as for back until 30 (30–32–32–34) sts remain above armhole. Shape neck: Continuing armhole shaping as established, leave center 18 (18–20–20–22) sts on holder for neck, and, working both sides at the same time, dec 1 st at neck edge of every other row 2 times. Continue armhole shaping until 1 st remains. Bind off.

SLEEVES: With size 3 needles and MC, cast on 28 (30–32–34–36) sts. Work in k 1, p 1 rib for 1½ inches, inc 6 sts evenly in last row to make 34 (36–38–40–42) sts. With size 5 needles, work as follows: reverse stockinette stitch on 10 (11–12–13–14) sts, pattern #4 on 14 sts, reverse stockinette stitch to end of row. Work as established, inc 1 st at each end every 1½ inches 5 (6–6–7–8) times to make 44 (48–50–54–58) sts. Work even until 10 (11–12–13–14) inches from beg, or desired length to underarm.

SHAPE ARMHOLE AND CAP: Bind off 2 (3–3–3–3) sts at beg of next 2 rows, then work armhole shaping as for back until 4 (4–4–6–6) sts remain. Leave on holder.

NECK BAND: Sew shoulder seams, leaving left front seam open if using zipper, left back seam open if not. Then, with right side facing, and using size 3 needles, work across sts from all holders and pick up and k 9 sts on each side of front neck. Work on these 66 (66–70–70–78) sts in k 1, p 1 rib for 1 inch. Bind off loosely in rib.

FINISHING: Sew underarm and side seams. If using zipper, sew in left front shoulder seam. If not, sew left back shoulder seam and side of neck band.

SAMPLER PULLOVER CHART

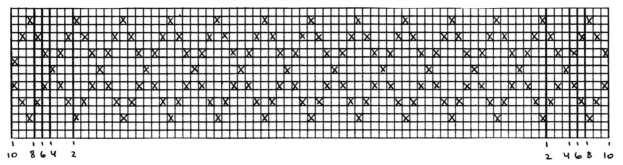

Girl's Wool and Mohair Coat

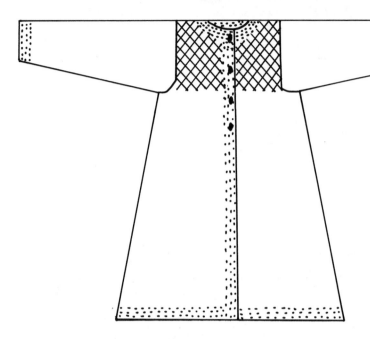

SIZES: Instructions are for size 12 months. Changes for sizes 2, 4, 6, 8, and 10 are in parentheses. Approximate chest measurements are 20 (22–24–25–26–28) inches.

MATERIALS: 7 (9–11–13–15–18) oz worsted weight Maine wool and 3 (4–5–6–7–9) oz worsted weight mohair, or 365 (470–575–680–785– 945) yds each. 1 pair each size 8 and size 10 needles or size needed to obtain gauge; 1 double-pointed needle (dpn); 4 ½-inch buttons.

GAUGE: Using 1 strand each Maine wool and mohair, 3.5 sts = 1 inch in stockinette stitch; 5 sts = 1 inch in honeycomb stitch.

NOTE: This coat is worked with 1 strand each wool and mohair held together throughout, or you can substitute a single strand of bulky weight wool.

STITCHES USED
Moss stitch
Row 1: K 1, p 1
Rows 2 and 4: K on k, p on p
Row 3: P 1, k 1

Honeycomb stitch
Row 1: Sl 1 st to dpn and hold in back of work, k 1, k 1 from dpn, sl 1 st to dpn and hold in front of work, k 1, k 1 from dpn.
Rows 2 and 4: Purl.
Row 3: Sl 1 st to dpn and hold in front of work, k 1, k 1 from dpn, sl 1 st to dpn and hold in back of work, k 1, k 1 from dpn.

BACK: With size 8 needles, cast on 58 (64–72–74–76–82) sts. Then, with size 10 needles, work in moss stitch for 1¼ inches. Continue in stockinette stitch (k 1 row, p 1 row) until 12 (14–16–19–21–24) inches from beg, or desired length to underarm.

SHAPE BACK ARMHOLE: With right side facing, bind off 3 sts at beg of next 2 rows, evenly dec 12 (16–20–16–16–18) sts in wrong-side row to leave 40 (42–46–52–54–58) sts. Then, begin working yoke in honeycomb stitch, keeping first and last st in stockinette stitch. Work even until 4¼ (4¾–5½–5¾–6–6¼) inches above start of yoke.

SHAPE SHOULDER: On next right-side row, bind off 13 (14–15–17–18–19) sts, leave next 14 (14–16–18–18–20) sts on holder for back of neck, bind off remaining sts.

LEFT FRONT: With size 8 needles, cast on 32 (35–39–40–41–44) sts. Then, with size 10 needles, work in moss stitch for 1¼ inches. Continue in stockinette stitch on 27 (30–34–35–36–39) sts, moss stitch on 5 sts for button band. Work as established until same length as back to underarm.

SHAPE FRONT ARMHOLE: With right side facing, bind off 3 sts at beg of next row. Then, on a wrong-side row, evenly dec 7 (8–10–9–8–9) sts across to leave 22 (24–26–28–30–32) sts, making sure not to work any decreases in band. On next right-side row, work in stockinette stitch on first st, honeycomb stitch on 16 (18–20–22–24–26) sts, moss stitch on last 5 sts. Continue as established until 2¼ (2¾–3½–3¾–3¾–4) inches above start of yoke.

SHAPE NECK: At beg of next wrong-side row (neck edge), leave 5 (6–7–7–8–9) sts on holder, work across as established. Then, dec 1 st at neck edge every other row 4 times to leave 13 (14–15–17–18–19) sts. Work as established until armhole is same depth as back to shoulder. Bind off all sts.

RIGHT FRONT: Work as for left front, reversing shaping and working 4 buttonholes (worked in band as follows: work 2 sts, yo, k 2 tog, work to last st) spaced 1¾ (2–2¼–2½–2½–2¾) inches apart. Plan to have top buttonhole in center of 1¼-inch-wide neck band. (Lowest buttonhole will be worked about waist-high.)

SLEEVES: With size 8 needles, cast on 20 (22–26–26–28–32) sts. With size 10 needles, work in moss stitch for 1¼ inch, then continue in stockinette stitch, inc 1 st at each end every 3 (4–4–3–3½–4) inches 2 (2–2–3–3–3) times to make 24 (26–30–32–34–38) sts. Work even until 7½ (9½–11–12–13–14) inches from beg, or desired length to underarm.

SHAPE ARMHOLE AND CAP: Bind off 3 sts at beg of next 2 rows, then 1 st at each end of every other row until 10 sts remain. Then, bind off 2 sts at beg of next 5 rows.

NECK BAND: Sew shoulder seams. With right side facing and using size 8 needles, work in moss stitch across 5 (6–7–7–8–9) sts from front holder, pick up and k 9 (9–9–9–10–10) sts on side of neck, work across 14 (14–16–18–18–20) sts from back holder, pick up and k 9 (9–9–9–10–10) sts on side of neck, work across 5 (6–7–7–8–9) sts from front holder. Work on these 42 (44–48–50–54–58) sts in moss stitch, making sure to work last buttonhole where required. Bind off all sts in rib when band is 1¼ inches wide.

FINISHING: Set in sleeves. Sew underarm and side seams. Sew buttons opposite buttonholes.

Boy's Placket Neck Pullover

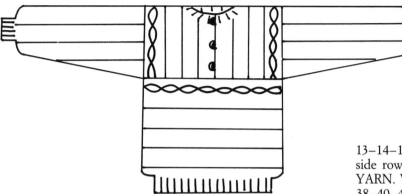

SIZES: Instructions are for size 12 months. Changes for sizes 2, 4, 6, 8, 10, and 12 are in parentheses. Finished chest measurements are 20 (22–24–25–26–28–30) inches.

MATERIALS: 6 (7–9–10–11–13–15) oz or 190 (245–315–350–385–445–510) yds bulky weight Maine wool. 1 pair each size 8 and size 10 needles or size needed to obtain gauge; 1 16-inch size 8 circular needle; 1 double-pointed needle (dpn), 1 size G crochet hook; 2 (2–2–3–3–3–3) ¾-inch buttons.

GAUGE: 3.5 sts = 1 inch in slipped rib pattern.

STITCHES USED
Slipped rib pattern
Row 1: *K 4, sl 1*, repeat between * across, end with k 4.
Row 2: Purl.
Cable (worked on 8 sts)
Rows 1 and 3: P 2, k 4, p 2.
Row 2 and all even rows: K 2, p 4, k 2.
Row 5: P 2, sl 2 to dpn and hold in front of work, k 2, k 2 from dpn, p 2.
Rows 7 and 9: Same as rows 1 and 3.
Repeat these 10 rows for cable.

NOTE: Lower half of sweater is worked from side to side rather than from cuff up.

BODY: With size 10 needles, beginning at side edge, cast on 22 (27–27–32–32–32–37) sts. Work as follows: Cable on 8 sts, slipped rib pattern to end of row. Work as established until 10 (11–12–12½–

13–14–15) inches from beg, ready to work a right-side row. Bind off all sts loosely. DO NOT CUT YARN. With size 8 needles, pick up and k 32 (36–38–40–42–46–48) sts on lower edge of piece for ribbing. Work in k 1, p 1 rib for 1 (1–2–1–1½–2–1) inches. Bind off all sts loosely in rib. Work an identical piece for other side of body.

BACK YOKE: Using size 10 needles and with right side facing, pick up and k 35 (40–40–45–45–50–55) sts along top edge (cable edge) of back. Beginning with row 2 of both stitches (wrong side facing), work as follows: Cable on 8 sts, slipped rib pattern to last 8 sts, cable on 8 sts. Work as established until yoke measures 4 (4½–5–5¼–5½–6–6½) inches. On next right-side row, bind off 11 (13–13–15–15–17–19) sts, leave next 13 (14–14–15–15–16–17) sts on holder for back of neck, bind off remaining sts.

LEFT FRONT YOKE: Using size 10 needles and with right side facing, pick up and k 17 (20–20–22–22–25–27) sts from left edge of front to center of front (left half of yoke). With wrong side facing, work as follows, beginning with row 2 of both stitches: Slipped rib pattern to last 8 sts, cable on 8 sts. Work as established until yoke measures 2½ (3–3–3¼–3½–4–4) inches.

SHAPE NECK: On next wrong-side row, leave 3 (4–4–4–4–5–5) sts on holder at neck edge, then dec 1 st at same edge every other row 3 times. Work even on remaining 11 (13–13–15–15–17–19) sts as established until same length as back to shoulder. Bind off all sts.

RIGHT FRONT YOKE: With size 10 needles, cast on 3 sts, then with right side facing, pick up and k 17 (20–20–22–22–25–27) sts from center edge of front to right edge of front. With wrong side facing, work as follows, beginning with row 2 of both stitches: Cable on 8 sts, slipped rib pattern to end of row. Work as established until yoke measures 2½ (3–3–3¼–3½–4–4) inches.

SHAPE NECK: On next right-side row, leave 6 (7–7–7–7–8–8) sts on holder at neck edge, then dec 1 st at same edge every other row 3 times. Finish this side as for left front.

SLEEVES: Sew shoulder seams. With right side facing and using size 10 needles, pick up and k 29 (31–34–36–39–41–46) sts. Purl across. Next row, work as follows: k 0 (1–0–1–0–1–1) st, slipped rib pattern on next 29 (29–34–34–39–39–44) sts, end with k 0 (1–0–1–0–1–1) st. Work as established, dec 1 st at each end every 1¼ (1¼–1¼–1¼–1½–1¼–1¼) inches 5 (6–6–7–7–8 –9) times to leave 19 (19–22–22–25–25–28) sts, until sleeve measures 6½ (8½–9½–10½–11½–12–13) inches, decreasing 3 (3–4–4–3–3–4) sts evenly in last row to leave 16 (16–18–18–22–22–24) sts. Then, with size 8 needles, work in k 1, p 1 rib for 1 (1–1½–1½–1½–2–2) inches. Bind off all sts loosely in rib.

NECK BAND: With right side facing and using circular needle, work across 6 (7–7–7–7–8–8) sts from right front holder, pick up and k 8 (8–10–10–10–10–13) sts on side of neck, work across 13 (14–14–15–15–16–17) sts from back holder, pick up and k 8 (9–11–10–10–11–13) sts on side of neck, work across 3 (4–4–4–4–5–5) sts from left front holder. Work on these 38 (42–46–46–46–50–56) sts in k 1, p 1, rib for ¾ inch. Bind off all sts in rib.

FINISHING: With crochet hook, work 1 row of single crochet on right and left front edges of yoke center opening, evenly spacing 2 (2–2–3–3–3–3) chain-2 buttonloops on left edge only. Lap left front over right and slip-stitch lower edge of right front to inside. Sew buttons.

Girl's Daisy Cardigan

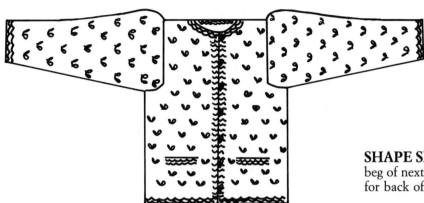

SIZES: Instructions are for size 3. Changes for sizes 8 and 12 are in parentheses. Finished chest measurements are 23¼ (27½–30¼) inches.

MATERIALS: 9 (11–13) oz or 480 (585–690) yds worsted weight Maine wool. 1 pair each size 4 and size 6 needles or size needed to obtain gauge; 1 crochet hook size G; 6 (7–7) ½-inch buttons.

GAUGE: 4.5 sts = 1 inch in Daisy Stitch.

STITCHES USED
Garter stitch K every row.
Daisy stitch
Rows 1 and 5: Knit.
Row 2 and all wrong side rows: Purl.
Row 3: *K 5, p 3 tog, leave on needle, yo, p same 3 tog again (for daisy)*. Repeat between *, end with K 5.
Row 7: K 1, *work daisy as in row 3, k 5*. Repeat between *, end with k 1 instead of k 5.
Repeat these 8 rows for pattern.

BACK: With size 4 needles, cast on 50 (58–66) sts. Work in garter stitch for 8 rows, inc 3 sts evenly in last row to make 53 (61–69) sts. Then, with size 6 needles, work in daisy stitch until 9½ (10½–11½) inches from beg.

SHAPE ARMHOLE: Bind off 3 sts at beg of next 2 rows, then dec 1 st at each end of every other row 2 (3–4) times to leave 43 (49–55) sts. Work even until 5 (5½–6½) inches above armhole.

SHAPE SHOULDER: Bind off 13 (15–18) sts at beg of next row, leave next 17 (19–19) sts on holder for back of neck, bind off remaining sts.

POCKET LINING (make 2): With size 6 needles, cast on 14 sts. Work in stockinette stitch (k 1 row, p 1 row) for 3 inches. Leave sts on holder.

RIGHT FRONT: With size 4 needles, cast on 25 (31–33) sts. Work in garter stitch for 8 rows, inc 1 st in last row to make 26 (32–34) sts. Then, with size 6 needles, work in garter stitch on 5 (3–5) sts, then in daisy stitch on 21 (29–29) sts until 3½ inches from beg. On next right-side row, work as established on 6 (9–10) sts, work in garter stitch on next 14 sts for pocket welt, work as established to end of row. Repeat this row 5 more times. On next right-side row, work to pocket welt, bind off 14 sts, work to end of row. With wrong side facing, work to bound-off sts, work across the 14 sts left on holder for one pocket lining, work to end of row. Work even, shaping armhole at left edge as for back until 3 (3½–4½) inches above armhole.

SHAPE NECK: At neck edge, leave 5 (8–6) sts on holder, then dec 1 st at same edge every other row 3 times to leave 13 (15–18) sts. Work even until same depth as back to shoulder. Bind off all sts.

LEFT FRONT: With size 4 needles, cast on 29 (35–37) sts. Work in garter stitch for 8 rows, inc 1 st in last row to make 30 (36–38) sts. Then, with size 6 needles, work in daisy stitch on 21 (29–29) sts, in garter stitch on 9 (7–9) sts. Work as established, making pocket welt and shaping armhole as for right front. Work even until ready to shape neck: At neck edge, leave 9 (12–10) sts on holder and complete neck and shoulder shaping as for right front.

SLEEVES: With size 4 needles, cast on 37 (37–45) sts. Work in garter stitch for 8 rows. Then, with size 6 needles, work in daisy stitch, inc 1 st at each end every 2 inches 1 (3–2) times to make 39 (43–49) sts, working inc sts in daisy stitch as required. Work even until 11 (13–15) inches from beg, or desired length to underarm.

SHAPE ARMHOLE AND CAP: Bind off 3 sts at beg of next 2 rows. Then, work even on these 33 (37–43) sts in daisy stitch until 4 (4½–5½) inches above armhole. On next right-side row, *k 3 tog* across, repeat between *, end with k 0 (1–1) to leave 11 (13–15) sts. Purl back. Then, *k 3 tog* across, end with k 2 tog (k 1–k 0). Bind off remaining 4 (5–5) sts.

NECK BAND: Sew shoulder seams. With right side facing and using size 4 needles, work across 5 (8–6) sts from right front holder, pick up and k 12 sts on side of neck, work across 17 (19–19) sts from back holder, pick up and k 12 sts on side of neck, work across 9 (12–10) sts from left front holder. Work on these 55 (63–59) sts in garter stitch for 8 rows. Bind off all sts.

FINISHING: With crochet hook, work 1 row of single crochet on right front edge, evenly spacing 6 (7–7) chain-2 buttonloops. Then, overlapping right front over left, mark places where buttons ought to go and sew them in place. Set in sleeves at shoulder. Sew underarm and side seams. Sew pocket linings in place.

Cabled Turtleneck

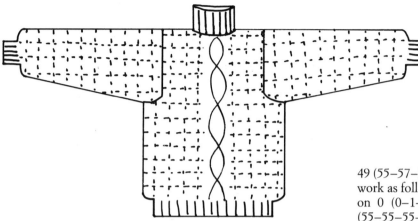

SIZES: Instructions are for size 2. Changes for sizes 4, 6, 8, 10, and 12 are in parentheses. Finished chest measurements are 22 (24–25–26½–28–30) inches.

MATERIALS: 7 (10–12–13–15–17) oz or 350 (500–600–650–750–850) yds worsted weight wool blend. 1 pair each size 5 and size 7 needles or size needed to obtain gauge; 1 set size 5 double-pointed needles (dpn).

GAUGE: 4.5 sts = 1 inch in square stitch.

STITCHES USED
Square stitch
Row 1 and all right-side rows: Knit.
Rows 2, 4, 6: K 1, *p 5, k 1*. Repeat between * across.
Row 8: *K 1, p 1*. Repeat between * across.
Repeat these 8 rows for pattern.
Cable

Row 1: P 2, k 9, p 2.
Row 2: K 2, p 9, k 2.
Row 3: P 2, sl next 3 sts to dpn and hold in front of work, k 3, k 3 from dpn, k 3, p 2.
Rows 4 and 6: As row 2.
Row 5: As row 1.
Row 7: P 2, k 3, sl next 3 sts to dpn and hold in back of work, k 3, k 3 from dpn, p 2.
Row 8: As row 2.
Repeat these 8 rows for pattern.

BACK: With size 5 needles, cast on 46 (52–54–56–60–64) sts. Work in k 1, p 1 rib for 1 (1½–1½–2–2–2) inches, inc 3 sts evenly in last row to make

49 (55–57–59–63–67) sts. Then, with size 7 needles, work as follows: Stockinette stitch (k 1 row, p 1 row) on 0 (0–1–2–1–0) sts, square stitch on next 49 (55–55–55–61–67) sts, stockinette stitch on any remaining stitches. Work as established, working row 8 of square stitch across the whole row for all sizes. Work in this manner until 8½ (9½–10–10½–11–11½) inches from beg, or desired length to underarm.

SHAPE ARMHOLE: Bind off 3 sts at beg of next 2 rows, then dec 1 st at each end of every other row 3 times to leave 37 (43–45–47–51–55) sts. Keeping pattern constant, work even until 4¾ (5–5¼–5½–6–6½) inches above armhole.

SHAPE SHOULDER: Bind off 10 (13–13–14–15–17) sts at beg of next row, leave next 17 (17–19–19–21–21) sts on holder for back of neck, bind off remaining sts.

FRONT: Work as for back until ribbing is complete. Then, with size 7 needles, work as follows: work in square stitch on 18 (21–22–23–25–27) sts, cable on 13 sts, square stitch to end of row. Care must be taken on rows 2, 4, and 6 of square stitch to position the centermost vertical ribs so that they will be at equal distances from the center cable. Work even, shaping armhole as for back until 2¼ (2½–2¾–3–3½–4) inches above armhole.

SHAPE NECK: Leave center 9 (9–11–11–13–13) sts on holder for front of neck, then, working both sides at the same time, dec 1 st at neck edge every other row 4 times to leave 10 (13–13–14–15–17) sts. Bind off all sts when front is same length as back to shoulder.

SLEEVES: With size 5 needles, cast on 22 (24–26–28–30–32) sts. Work in k 1, p 1 rib for 1 (1½–1½–1 ½–2–2) inches, inc 3 (7–5–3–7–5) sts evenly in last row to make 25 (31–31–31–37–37) sts. Then, with size 7 needles, work in square stitch, inc 1 st at each end every 1¾ (2–2–1¾–2–2) inches 5 (4–5–6–5–6) times to make 35 (39–41–43–47–49) sts, working these new sts in pattern as needed. Work even until 10 (11–12–13–14–15) inches from beg, or desired length to underarm. Bind off 3 sts at beg of next 2 rows, then dec 1 st at each end of every other row until 15 sts remain. Bind off 2 sts at beg of next 6 rows. Bind off remaining 3 sts.

COLLAR: Sew shoulder seams. With right side facing, using size 5 dpn needles and starting at left shoulder seam, pick up and k 17 sts on left side of neck, work across 9 (9–11–11–13–13) sts from front holder, pick up and k 17 sts on right side of neck, work across 17 (17–19–19–21–21) sts from back holder. Work on these 60 (60–64–64–68–68) sts in k 1, p 1 rib for 2½ (3–3½–3½–4–4½) inches. Bind off all sts loosely in rib.

FINISHING: Set in sleeves at shoulder. Sew underarm and side seams.

Tree of Life Pullover

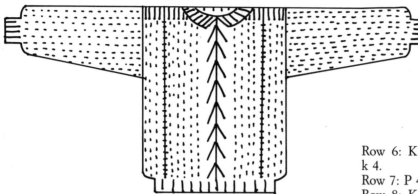

SIZES: Instructions are for size 2. Changes for sizes 4, 6, 8, 10, and 12 are in parentheses. Finished chest measurements are 22¼ (24½–25¾–26¾–28–30¼) inches.

MATERIALS: 8 (10–11–12–14–15) oz or 275 (340–375–410–475–510) yds bulky weight Maine wool. 1 pair each size 8 and size 10½ needles or size needed to obtain gauge. 1 16-inch size 8 circular needle and 1 double-pointed needle (dpn).

GAUGE: 3.5 sts = 1 inch in seed stitch.

STITCHES USED
Seed stitch
Row 1: K 1, p 1. Row 2: P on k, k on p. Repeat these 2 rows for pattern.
Barred rib
Row 1: P 2, keeping yarn in front, sl 1 as if to p, p 2. Row 2: K 2, p 1, k 2.
Repeat these two rows for pattern.
Tree of Life
Row 1: P 2, k 1, p 4, sl 1 with yarn in back (wyib), p 4, k 1, p 2.
Row 2: K 2, sl 1 with yarn in front (wyif), k 4, p 1, k 4, sl 1 wyif, k 2.
Row 3: P 2, [sl 1 to dpn and hold in front of work, p 1, k 1 from dpn (front cross: FC)], p 3, sl 1 wyib, p 3, [sl 1 to dpn and hold in back of work, k 1, p 1 from dpn (back cross: BC)], p 2.
Row 4: K 3, sl 1 wyif, k 3, p 1, k 3, sl 1 wyif, k 3.
Row 5: P 3, FC, p 2, sl 1 wyib, p 2, BC, p 3.

Row 6: K 4, sl 1 wyif, k 2, p 1, k 2, sl 1 wyif, k 4.
Row 7: P 4, FC, p 1, sl 1 wyib, p 1, BC, p 4.
Row 8: K 5, sl 1 wyif, k 1, p 1, k 1, sl 1 wyif, k 5.
Row 9: P 2, k 1, p 2, FC, sl 1 wyib, BC, p 2, k 1, p 2.
Row 10: K 2, sl 1 wyif, k 4, p 1, k 4, sl 1 wyif, k 2.
Repeat ROWS 3 THROUGH 10 ONLY for pattern.

BACK: With size 8 needles, cast on 38 (42–44–46–48–52) sts. Work in k 1, p 1 rib for 1½ (1½–1¾–1¾–2–2) inches, inc 1 st in last row to make 39 (43–45–47–49–53) sts. Then, with size 10½ needles, work in seed stitch on 3 (4–5–5–6–7) sts, barred rib on 5 sts, seed stitch on 4 (5–5–6–6–7) sts, Tree of Life on 15 sts, seed stitch on 4 (5–5–6–6–7) sts, barred rib on 5 sts, seed stitch on 3 (4–5–5–6–7) sts. Work as established until 8 (9½–10–10½–11–11½) inches from beg. Place markers on both ends for armhole. Continue as established until 2 (2½–2¾–3–3½–4) inches above markers. Then, work in k 1, p 1 rib for 2½ inches, making sure to k on k and p on p on wrong-side rows.

SHAPE SHOULDER: Bind off 13 (15–15–16–16–18) sts, leave next 13 (13–15–15–17–17) sts on holder for back of neck, bind off remaining sts.

FRONT: Work as for back until 2½ (3–3¼–3½–4–4½) inches above armhole markers. Shape neck: On next right-side row, leave center 9 (9–11–11–

KNITTED BY THEO HEALD

13–13) sts on holder. Then, working both sides at the same time, dec 1 st at neck edge of every other row 2 times to leave 13 (15–15–16–16–18) sts. Work as established until armhole is same depth as back to shoulder. Bind off all sts.

SLEEVES: Sew shoulder seams. With right side facing and size 10½ needles, pick up and k 32 (36–36–38–42–46) sts on armhole edge between markers. Work in seed stitch, decreasing 1 st at each end every 2½ (2¼–2½–2¾–2–1¾) inches 3 (4–4–4–6–7) times to leave 26 (28–28–30–30–32) sts. Work even until sleeve measures 8½ (10–11–12–13–14) inches from beg, decreasing 6 sts evenly in last row to leave 20 (22–22–24–24–26) sts. Then, with size 8 needles, work in k 1, p 1 rib for 1 inch. Bind off all sts.

COLLAR: With right side facing and using circular needle, divide sts on front holder evenly in 2, binding off center st. Work across 4 (4–5–5–6–6) sts from right side, pick up and k 12 sts on side of neck, work across 13 (13–15–15–17–17) sts from back holder, pick up and k 12 sts on side of neck, work across 4 (4–5–5–6–6) sts left on front holder. Work back and forth on these 45 (45–49–49–53–53) sts in k 1, p 1 rib for 2½ inches from beginning. With size 10½ needle, bind off all sts.

FINISHING: Sew underarm and side seams.

Bibliography

Some of the stitches used in this collection of my designs were extracted from the following books. These, and several other titles on the market, present an excellent collection of stitches and are a must for anyone who wishes to experiment with new designs.

Walker, Barbara. *A Treasury of Knitting Patterns.* Charles Scribner's Sons, New York, 1968.

1500 Patterns, no. 0J 84, Mon Tricot Collection. Cie des Editions de l'Alma, Paris, January 1984 edition.